$45.00

D0889683

Bloom's Modern Critical Interpretations

Bloom's Modern Critical Interpretations

Maya Angelou's
I Know Why the Caged Bird Sings
New Edition

Edited and with an introduction by
Harold Bloom
Sterling Professor of the Humanities
Yale University

BLOOM'S
LITERARY CRITICISM
An imprint of Infobase Publishing

Bloom's Modern Critical Interpretations:
Maya Angelou's *I Know Why the Caged Bird Sings*—New Edition
Copyright © 2009 by Infobase Publishing

Introduction © 2009 by Harold Bloom

Bloom's Literary Criticism
An imprint of Infobase Publishing
132 West 31st Street
New York NY 10001

Library of Congress Cataloging-in-Publication Data

Maya Angelou's *I Know Why the Caged Bird Sings* / edited and with an introduction by Harold Bloom.—New ed.
    p. cm.—(Bloom's Modern Critical Interpretations)
Includes bibliographical references and index.
ISBN 978-1-60413-187-1 (acid-free paper) 1. Angelou, Maya. I know why the caged bird sings. 2. African American authors—Biography—History and criticism. 3. African American entertainers—Biography—History and criticism. 4. African American women—Intellectual life. I. Bloom, Harold.

PS3551.N464Z77 2009
818'.5409—dc22
                              2009012580

You can find Bloom's Literary Criticism on the World Wide Web at
http://www.chelseahouse.com.

Cover design by Ben Peterson

Printed in the United States of America
MP BCL 10 9 8 7 6 5 4 3 2 1

This book is printed on acid-free paper.

Contents

Editor's Note

My introduction praises Angelou's achieved tone in her prose, which is at once intimate and serene.

As there are fourteen essays and interviews fused together here, I will forgo discussing them individually and instead I will seek to sum up their combined effect upon me, as their reader. Humor and strength of character are the dominant emphases, as should be expected of Maya Angelou. Whether she speaks for herself, or in the reflection of others, we hear a hard-won wisdom of self-acceptance and an extraordinary compassion forged out of suffering and endurance.

HAROLD BLOOM

Introduction

African American autobiography is now a much-studied mode, as befits a tradition that includes such important works as Frederick Douglass's *Narrative* of 1845, Richard Wright's *Black Boy,* Alex Haley's *Autobiography of Malcolm X,* and the ongoing sequence of memoirs by Maya Angelou. Critics have agreed on the importance of the slave narrative and the African American church sermon as sources for this tradition, but I suspect that Angelou, in particular, is highly eclectic, and draws upon a very wide range of influences. The buoyant intensity of her tone, at once intimate and serene, is one of her principal virtues as an autobiographer, and her fictions of the self doubtless will maintain that attractive tone, which brings her an immense variety of readers.

Angelou tells us that she read widely as a child, saving her "young and loyal passion" for the African American poets Paul Laurence Dunbar, Langston Hughes, and James Weldon Johnson, all of whose voices can still be heard in her own poetry. Dunbar, whom she cites first, provided her with her most famous title, in the final stanza of his High Romantic lyric, "Sympathy," which still impresses me as a poignant and vital poem:

> I know what the caged bird feels, alas!
> When the sun is bright on the upland slopes;
> When the wind stirs soft through the springing grass,
> And the river flows like a stream of glass;
> When the first bird sings and the first bud opes,
> And the faint perfume from its chalice steals—
> I know what the caged bird feels!

1

I know why the caged bird beats his wing
Till its blood is red on the cruel bars;
For he must fly back to his perch and cling
When he fain would be on the bough a-swing;
And a pain still throbs in the old, old scars
And they pulse again with a keener sting—
I know why he beats his wing!
I know why the caged bird sings, ah me,
When his wing is bruised and his bosom sore,—
When he beats his bars and he would be free;
It is not a carol of joy or glee,
But a prayer that he sends from his heart's deep core,
But a plea, that upward to Heaven he flings—
I know why the caged bird sings!

I find it extraordinary that Angelou's *I Know Why the Caged Bird Sings* is finally more a carol than it is a prayer or a plea. The young Marguerite Johnson (as Angelou then was named) tells a story that would necessarily sink most of us without trace, were it our own. Yet she is a survivor, and the tale of her first sixteen years is a litany of successful endurances. Like all autobiographies, it doubtless has fictive elements, but whatever they may be, they evidently work to reinforce the book's engaging artfulness. The strong pattern of the narrative takes Angelou from public and private humiliations and deprivations through the terror of being raped at the age of eight. Trauma ensues, and yet the extraordinarily strong soul of Marguerite Johnson eventually goes beyond the trauma. At sixteen, she becomes an unmarried mother, through choice, a high school graduate, and a fully individuated consciousness, capable of sustaining all the hazards yet to arrive.

I return to the question of the achieved tone of *I Know Why the Caged Bird Sings*. Few of us, in our actual lives, can speak both intimately and serenely to others. Angelou, in her first memoir, provides us with a voice that we encounter very infrequently, whether in life or in literature. Sometimes I can hear a touch of Kipling's tone in that voice, and I suspect that Angelou has learned from Kipling's great tale, *Kim*, something of the knack of balancing closeness and detachment. Intimacy, in a woman autobiographer, necessarily has very different aspects than in a male storyteller, and yet Angelou, like Kipling, is very much a performer. Something in her, as in him, resembles a tale-spinner in a bazaar, directly confronting an audience. To accomplish the paradox of being there with the reader, and yet maintaining a reserve, both in regard to audience and to self, is a considerable achievement. I have doubts about Angelou's poetry, and do not find her other memoirs as compelling as her first, but *I Know Why the Caged Bird Sings* is likely to keep its vast readership for some years to come.

LUCINDA H. MACKETHAN

Mother Wit: Humor in Afro-American Women's Autobiography

The expression "Mother Wit" has three associations: according to Alan Dundes, it is, first, "a popular term in black speech referring to common sense"; secondly, it is "the kind of good sense not necessarily learned from books or in school"; and thirdly, "with its connotation of collective wisdom acquired by the experience of living and from generations past," it is "often expressed in folklore" (Dundes xiv). In his collection of essays related to Afro-American folklore, Dundes consistently pairs mother wit with laughter and humor, for, as he says, "it is what makes a people laugh that reveals the soul of that people" (611). When we look, however, at the word *mother*, in relation to mother wit, we might wonder how the term applies to the traditional experience of the Afro-American mother from slavery times forward; the question we could ask is, Why are these women laughing? A survey of three important autobiographical accounts of black women's existence in America, the works of Harriet Jacobs, Zora Neale Hurston, and Maya Angelou, reveals little cause for laughter. Jacobs' *Incidents in the Life of a Slave Girl*, the only woman's fugitive slave narrative verified as having been written by the slave herself, tells how Jacobs hid from her master for seven years in the narrow attic crawl space of her free grandmother's house in North Carolina; Hurston's *Dust Tracks on a Road* is in large part the story of a woman who succeeded in many ways but ultimately could not

Studies in American Humor, Volume 4, Numbers 1–2 (Spring–Summer 1985): pp. 51–61. © 1985 Lucinda H. MacKethan.

triumph over the poverty and sense of isolation that shadowed her from early childhood until her death in a county home and her burial in a segregated cemetery. Angelou's *I Know Why the Caged Bird Sings* contains the gruesome account of how Angelou, at age eight, was raped by her mother's lover; it ends with her attempts as a sixteen-year-old unwed mother to nurture and protect her newborn son.

These three autobiographies are case studies of what Elizabeth Schultz has named "the black American woman's struggle for survival and liberation . . . against the dual traditions of racism and sexism in America" (317). In Hurston's novel, *Their Eyes Were Watching God*, Janie Crawford's grandmother identifies the situation that all three works dramatize:

> "Honey, de white man is de ruler of everything as fur as Ah been able tuh find out. Maybe it's some place way off in de ocean where de black man is in power, but we don't know nothin' but what we see. white man throw down de load and tell de nigger man tuh pick it up. He pick it up because he have to, but he don't tote it. He hand it to his womenfolks. De nigger woman is de mule uh de world so fur as Ah can see." (29)

In this remark we hear echoed the words of Harriet Jacobs, remarking that "When they told me my new-born babe was a girl, my heart was heavier than it had ever been before. Slavery is terrible for men; but it is far more terrible for women" (Jacobs 110); perhaps too Hurston's thoughts on her own life went into the making of her grandmother character's words: in *Dust Tracks* she said, "I have been in Sorrow's kitchen and licked out all the pots" (Hurston 280). Maya Angelou's summation is most explicit: "The Black female," she said, "is assaulted in her tender years by all those common forces of nature at the same time that she is caught in the tripartite crossfire of masculine prejudice, white illogical hate and Black lack of power" (Angelou 231). Yet while Jacobs, Hurston, and Angelou all testify here to the truth of Janie Crawford's grandmother's words, what their autobiographies are about is the more important truth that if the black woman is the world's mule, she is, like Francis, at least a talking mule, and in her talk is the "mother wit" that is not so named for nothing: mother wit is the verbal weapon of survival that informs the experience in these works and makes them, finally, celebrations of "getting ovah," assertions of identity, proclamations of the beauty and mastery of circumstance that simply being Black and a woman can affirm.

The humor of mother wit in these three compelling versions of black female experience is the humor of the word as it has been deviously employed since slavery times by people denied access to all forms of power, but most particularly to the power of language: it was the skillful wielding of the word, in spiritual, folktale, and even harmless-seeming everyday conversation that gave the slaves their means of control over their masters. "Both in slavery times and now," Geneva Smitherman tells us, "the black community places a high value on the spoken word" (77). Slave narrators like Harriet Jacobs announced their triumphant mastery of the forbidden word through the daring act of writing out, and thereby enacting, their lives as freepeople. Hurston, out of her love for Afro-American folk expression, harnessed the word to the essential act of transcribing the vital sources of her culture; Angelou's story of her girlhood is in many places a lyrical testament to language as providing her one saving image of self; from a childhood in which she tried to live wordlessly as a means of protecting herself against knowledge that was certain pain, Angelou emerged armed, she says, with a "secret word which called forth the djinn who was to serve me all my life: books" (170).

The woman's brand of mother wit that we see in the works of Jacobs, Hurston, and Angelou is tied to their special sense of the capacities of language as an enabling power. That power first reveals itself in the humor of caricature, in broad slaps of ridicule applied to the backsides of oppressors who include white men, white women, and black men too. Secondly, the power of language appears in the humor of exaggeration, a device which comes into play particularly when these women writers portray the gulf that existed between what they had the right to expect and what the world was willing to allow. And finally, the power of mother wit resides perhaps most plentifully in their representations of their own mothers' words of wisdom; in all three works mother figures offer the practical, loving, yet also tough and disciplining advice for life that they know their black daughters must acquire if they are to have any hope of being more than the mules of the world. Jacobs' portrayal of her grandmother, Hurston's memories of the mother whose death altered her childhood course forever, Angelou's characterizations of both her mother and grandmother seem to enact in several ways Alice Walker's idea that "our mothers and grandmothers have, more often than not anonymously, handed on the creative spark, the seed of the flower they themselves never hoped to see" (Walker 240). Thus for all their shadows, the mother and mother-wit stories of Jacobs, Hurston, and Angelou are not tragedies; they are comic in their use of word play, caricature, and exaggeration and in their affirmation of what their mothers have handed down: "respect for the possibilities," as Alice Walker puts it, "and the will to grasp them" (Walker 242).

Harriet Jacobs' autobiography, *Incidents in the Life of a Slave Girl,* uses caricature and exaggeration as tools of invective to bring in the judgment of her very specifically targeted audience, "the women of the North," against the master class of the South. Her own master and mistress in Edenton, North Carolina, are frequently lampooned and in that way are effectively dehumanized. The master, Dr. Flint, is a villain figure of sentimental novel vintage, and while there is nothing laughable about his lust or his cruelty, he himself is a uniformly ineffectual Lothario; in his jealous rages he hisses like a snake, springs "like a wolf," and storms about like "a restless spirit from the pit." "Satan had no difficulty determining the color of his soul," we are told (Jacobs 541).

Yet Dr. Flint never had his way with Linda Brent, as Jacobs calls herself in her narrative. In order to foil his attempts to force her into bed, Jacobs allowed the attentions of another white townsman and bore two children by him. When Dr. Flint threatened these children, who "followed the condition of the mother," Jacobs ran away, but only as far as her grandmother's house. There, for seven years, her relatives managed to keep her hidden, even from her own children who lived below. In a crawlspace only three feet high, she suffered from the cold and heat, from insect bites and cramps; still this section of her narrative contains some finely ironic scenes that Jacobs herself saw as a comedy. It pleased her to exhibit a thwarted Dr. Flint, who often visited her grandmother to vent his rage that his Linda had made her escape to the North; little did he know that she was listening just above his head. How he was tricked into believing in her disappearance is a lesson in the power that literacy conferred on the slave as well as a prime example of mother wit. Because she could read and write, Jacobs was able to concoct letters to the Doctor that would make him think she was living in New York. She included references to authentic street names and numbers that she gleaned from an old New York newspaper, and a friend carried the letters north for her, where they were mailed at intervals back to the master in North Carolina. Taking the bait, Dr. Flint would appear at the grandmother's door, often twisting what was in the letters to try to make the old woman think that Linda longed to return home. "This was as good as a comedy to me, who heard it all," writes Jacobs. For years she could enjoy watching her old tormentor's futile searches through New York and Massachusetts for his prized possession; her family tricked him, again, into selling her children to their father. Thus for all his constant ranting and raving, Dr. Flint never won in any contest with his female slave; as Jacobs remarks, "My master had power and law on his side; I had a determined will. There is might in each" (130).

One remarkable quality of *Incidents* is its presentation of a southern sisterhood which crossed racial and class lines to unite white and black women in a struggle against the tyranny of a patriarchal society. Only one woman is pictured as a cruel supporter of slavery, and that is Dr. Flint's wife, whose jealousy and indolence make her a classic shrew. Sarcasm is almost always present in Jacobs' descriptions of her:

> She had not the strength to superintend her household affairs; but her nerves were so strong, that she could sit in her easy chair and

see a woman whipped, till the blood trickled from every stroke of the lash. . . . If dinner was not served at the exact time on that particular Sunday, she would station herself in the kitchen, and wait till it was dished, and then spit in all the kettles and pans that had been used for cooking. She did this to prevent the cook and her children from eking out their meagre fare with the remains of the gravy and other scrapings. (22)

When she learned of her husband's interest in Linda, Mrs. Flint took the girl to sleep in her own compartments, where, we are told, she spent "many a sleepless night to watch over me" (54). Sometimes, Jacobs says, "she whispered in my ear, as though it was her husband speaking to me, and listened to hear what I would answer." Thus Mrs. Flint is reduced to a laughable cartoon of the jealous wife, driven to crawling along the floor in the dark, hoping to catch her husband and slave in "the act." While her husband was busy wooing Linda with the promise that he would make a lady of her, the lady of the house stood guard, like a surly dog, over her slave's virtue.

Jacobs' tale is a somber one, relieved only infrequently by these cartoons of the master and mistress and sometimes by the use of dialogue in which the slave's and the master's intelligence and sensitivity are contrasted through their speech. Jacobs' battle of wits against her master is a battle of words—his rage against her cool sarcasm, as when he grills her about her white lover: "'Do you love him?' said he, in a hissing tone. 'I am thankful that I do not despise him,'" Linda replies. In another scene she relates a confrontation between her grandmother and a group of rowdy poor whites who had been empowered, during the weeks following the Nat Turner uprising, with the right to search homes of blacks for evidence of insurrection. At her grandmother's house, one ruffian, speaking barely decipherable English, asks, "Where'd the damned niggers get all dis sheet an' table clarf?" The grandmother, in a rare display of. sass, retorts, "You may be sure we didn't pilfer 'em from your houses" (100). The men leave, stymied by the black woman's word wielding, a power that humiliates them without ever challenging their authority.[1]

Jacobs' grandmother, very much like Maya Angelou's later, was a strong, nurturing presence who yet constantly counselled forbearance rather than rebellion, endurance instead of escape. While these two almost archetypal figures never openly challenged the double burden of racial and sexual prejudice that they were forced as black women to bear, both exude an unshakable dignity, an inner faith in their ability to prevail where it mattered most—in the preservation of their self-respect. Jacobs tells us that it was at her grandmother's house that she learned the words that carried her to freedom: "He that is *willing* to be a slave, let him be a slave." The grandmother lived long enough to see Linda Brent make her way to New York, where she was finally able to secure her and her children's freedom. Jacobs closes the book that she published in 1861 with thoughts of the woman who made the painful recollections of her past possible to bear.

Jacobs' autobiography ends with the image of home and family, with the writer's journey successfully ended in the freedom to be the mother and homemaker that the grandmother's life idealized for her. Simply in its title, Hurston's *Dust Tracks on a Road* indicates the great distance that separated not so much the wills or needs of women of the two different periods but their starting points, their directions, and their audiences. For Jacobs the road was something to leave behind, for Hurston something to embrace in a new challenge against different kinds of chains binding black women in the America of the early decades of the twentieth century. The most vibrant and least ambivalent section of Hurston's autobiography pictures her childhood years in Eatonton, Florida, a small southern town yet one light years removed from the Edenton, N.C., of Jacobs' time. Eatonton, Hurston tells us, was "a pure Negro town—charter, mayor, council, town marshal, and all" (Hurston 3), and her father was a three-term mayor who wrote the town laws. In her early years, then, she was surrounded by people who had a sense of their own importance—Eatonton was like an oasis in the desert of the South, and Hurston was bound to have imbibed some of its confidence. From her mother she received the encouragement to be the kind of woman that Harriet Jacobs became only in the face of tremendous opposition: Hurston remembers that "Mama exhorted her children at every opportunity to 'jump at de sun'.... She conceded that I was impudent and given to talking back, but she didn't want to 'squinch my spirit' too much for fear that I would be a mealy-mouthed rag doll by the time I got grown" (21). In her self-presentation, Hurston begins then with the assurance that she *should* be somebody: "Zora is my young 'un," her mother insisted, predicting that she would "come out more than conquer" specifically through the "sassy tongue" that everyone else deplored.

Hurston sets up the events of *Dust Tracks'* early chapters to target the three moving spirits in her life: a love of language pinned to a sense of the magic of the things of the world; wanderlust, an urge for the road that her mother could only explain as the result of a conjure; and differentness, a belief that her stars decreed that she would never be like those around her, both because she was always looking for the extraordinary in experience and because she trusted mysterious visions that told her of her destiny. It would be language and wit that provided the continuity for the lonely picaro existence that Hurston defined as her fate. The form of wit that seemed to come most naturally was a comic sense of the disparity between desires and realities— her own and others. Speaking of her childhood dissatisfaction with life, she writes, "Stew beef, fried fat-back and morning grits were no ambrosia from Valhalla. Raking back yards and carrying chamber pots were not the tasks of Thor" (56). She used a folktale to poke fun at racial pretensions, relating a theory of how the black folks got black that was one of the many "lying stories" of the men who gathered at Joe Clarke's store: when God was giving out color to folks, the last ones to show up, being late for their appointment with the Almighty and afraid of missing their gift, crowded so close that the Old Maker hollered, "Git back! Git back!" But the folks misunderstood and thought He said, "Get black!" Thus, Hurston concludes, "they just got black, and kept the thing a going" (69).

This story appears both in an early chapter and again in one called "My People! My People!," which was originally written in 1937 and heavily edited when *Dust Tracks* was published in 1942. In the original version, the folktale ends Hurston's discussion of what it means to have every judgment and motive shaped by race consciousness, or to deny being "kinfolks" with "skinfolks" on the basis of race. Her last comment on the original version is that the folktale tells us that "we are no race. We are just a collection of people who overslept our time and got caught in the draft" (306). In both versions of "My People! My People!" (but much more in the original one), Hurston tells several racial jokes in order to confront both white and black racial attitudes: "I am the only Negro," she says at one point, "whose grandfather on the mother's side was *not* an Indian chief" (235). In the early version she announces several comic tests which might help one to recognize "My People!": most of the signs are derogatory, but one of them emphasizes her special sense of language: "If he hunts for six big words where one little one would do, that's My People. . . . Somebody didn't know the word total nor entire so they made bodacious. Then there's asterperious, and so on. When you find a man chewing up the dictionary and spitting out language, that's My People" (298). Such jokes are in-jokes, and most in this chapter indicate a level of irritation beneath the pose of tolerant acceptance. The jokes Negroes tell on themselves, Langston Hughes wrote in an essay of that title, constitute "the humor of frustration, and the laughter with which these sallies are greeted, for all its loudness, is a desperate laughter" (Hughes 639). In Hurston's case this point is underscored by what she wrote at the end of the edited version of "My People": "I maintain that I have been a Negro three times—a Negro baby, a Negro girl and a Negro woman" (237). The exasperated cry of "My People! My People!" might be an in-joke, but it is also, for Hurston, an announcement of either exclusiveness or exclusion that in any case denied her the individuality that she, particularly as Negro *girl* and Negro *woman,* found threatened all too often.

In one other area Hurston applied mother wit to puncture a particular pretension, the ideal of Love with a capital L. Again, her sense of her differentness, her problems with winning respect for her womanhood, and her eye for debunking delusions of grandeur make capital L Love a perfect target. The scene that she sets reflects the fact that in her own life, her work—her oath to "take the hard road of labor"—made her vulnerable to the sexist charge that she was unwomanly. Talking of types of lovers, Hurston first regales us with the one who "whisper[s] gustily into my ear" while "I may be thinking of turnip greens with dumplings, or more royalty checks, and here is a man who visualizes me on a divan sending the world up in smoke" (262). "There must be something about me that looks sort of couchy," she concludes. Another lover-type is the one who makes her feel "the divine urge for an hour, a day or maybe a week. Then it is gone and my interest returns to corn pone and mustard greens, or rubbing a paragraph with a soft cloth" (264). Her conclusion: "much that passes for constant love is a golded-up moment walking in its sleep. Some people know that it is the walk of the dead, but in desperation and desolation they have staked everything on life after death and the resurrection, so they haunt the graveyard" (264–265).

One of Hurston's most colorful characters is also one of the most gifted, in her experience, of those who could do what she called "specifying," a kind of "signifying" or word-wit that embeds insult and reversal of status in adroit power-plays with language. Hurston's champion in this skill is Big Sweet, a tough saw-mill town Mama who was engaged, when Huston met her, in bringing a man in the street "up to date on his ancestry": she "broke the news to him, in one of her mildest bulletins, that his pa was double-humped camel and his ma was a grass-gut cow. . . . He was a bitch's baby out of a buzzard egg" (187). Here is a woman using mother wit in a age-old manner, to bring the power of the word into the arsenal of the once weaker and more abused group—Big Sweet is good at pistols and knives, but best in what Hurston and other Afro-American woman autobiographers recognize as their most effective defense in a world where, as Hurston put it, "that white man could run faster," and "My grandma . . . being the pursued, had to look back over her shoulder every now and then to see how she was doing" (236).

The development of verbal humor as a survival strategy, which Jacobs tried tentatively and Hurston celebrated boisterously, is a unifying device for the events of her life that Maya Angelou selected for *I Know Why the Caged Bird Sings*. Angelou the autobiographer takes her childhood self, who goes by many names, on a kind of quest for a name and for words. The book's first scene is comic as well as pathetic: in the Colored Methodist Episcopal Church, young Margeurite Johnson cannot call up the words she is supposed to say in the Easter pageant; at the scene's end, she runs from the church, looking (to herself) a ridiculous figure in lavender taffeta, wetting her pants, laughing to be free from the agonizing turmoil of having to depend on the words of others. The progress of this girl's life is made possible by a series of word-bringers—her brother, her teachers, her mother's con men friends, her mother herself—who gradually open to her the potential of language; words alone can free her from her fear of and dependency on others' conceptions.

Thus, with no ability to raise the words she needs, Margeurite in the first scene is betrayed by the white world's view of beauty: "Because I was really white," she tries to think, "and because a cruel fairy stepmother, who was understandably jealous of my beauty, had turned me into a too-big Negro girl, with nappy black hair, broad feet, and a space between her teeth that would hold a number-two pencil"(2). By the end of the book, Maya is not only talking but she has an edge on her white school mates; she and her friends "were alert to the gap separating the written word from the colloquial. We learned to slide out of one language and into another without being conscious of the effort"(191).

The most important of the word-bringers in Maya's life is her mother—a savvy, sassy, street-wise Mama who makes Black beautiful and language a gift of the body as well as an art of the mind. Vivian Baxter Johnson can dance, can shoot a crooked business partner, can make her living in the tough blues joints of St. Louis and San Francisco. Yet most of all she can talk, and unlike Maya's conservative southern grandmother's, her talk is full of hope, irreverence for tradition, and scorn for anyone who thinks they can keep her down. When she repeats the old report, "They tell me the whitefolks still in the lead," she says it, Angelou tells us, "as if that was not quite the whole truth" (175). Vivian's words are a compendium of mother wit: "She had a store of aphorisms," Angelou remarks, "which she dished out as the occasion demanded" (228): "The Man upstairs, He don't make mistakes" (237); "It ain't no trouble when you pack double" (229); "Nothing beats a trial but a failure" (225); and perhaps most to our point, "Sympathy is next to shit in the dictionary, and I can't even read" (175).

While we are given no explicit statement at the end of her story that Margeurite Johnson has fully absorbed what she needs of her mother's verbal capacities, Maya's own nascent motherhood, and her attitude toward becoming a mother, indicate that a survivor is coming into being. She tells us her feelings as a young, unwed mother who managed to hide her pregnancy from her family for almost eight months, and her words have a kind of triumph in them: "I had a baby. He was beautiful and mine. Totally mine. No one had bought him for me. No one had helped me endure the sickly gray months. I had had help in the child's conception, but no one could deny that I had had an immaculate pregnancy" (245). Gone is the girl who could see her Blackness only as some cruel fairy godmother's revenge. With a real mother, and mother wit, Maya has the preparation she needs to become the writer, the word-bringer, who created *I Know Why the Caged Bird Sings*.

One joke that the Black American community has shared for a long time shows a young black girl gazing into the fabled mirror to ask, "Who's the fairest of all?," whereupon the mirror, of course, answers back: "It's Snow White, you Black bitch, and don't you forget it." The joke, we can bet, is a trick on that tired white trope, locked as it is in the blind and self-reflexive looking glass of impotent white hate. The autobiographies of Harriet Jacobs, Zora Neale Hurston, and Maya Angelou reveal that, beginning in slavery times, women found the means, in the company of other nurturing women, to change the joke and slip the yoke. So indeed, they don't call it Mother Wit for nothing.

NOTE

'A valuable discussion of Jacobs' dialogues appears in William Andrews' forthcoming book, *Afro-American Autobiography, The First 100 Years* (University of Illinois Press).

WORKS CITED

Angelou, Maya. *I Know Why the Caged Bird Sings.* New York: Bantam Books, 1971.

Dundes, Alan. *Mother Wit From the Laughing Barrel.* Englewood Cliffs, N.J.: Prentice-Hall, 1973.

Hurston, Zora Neale. *Dust Tracks on a Road.* 2nd ed., with intro by Robert E. Hemenway. Chicago: University of Illinois Press, 1984.

———. *Their Eyes Were Watching God.* Chicago: University of Illinois Press, 1978.

Hughes, Langston. "Jokes Negroes Tell on Themselves." In *Mother Wit from the Laughing Barrel.* Englewood Cliffs, N.J.: Prentice-Hall, 1973, 637–641.

Jacobs, Harriet. *Incidents in the Life of a Slave Girl.* Written by herself. Miami, Fla.: Mnemosyne Publishing Co., 1969.

Schultz, Elizabeth, "Free in Fact and at Last: The Image of the Black Woman in Black American Fiction." In *What Manner of Woman: Essays on English and American Life and Literature.* New York University Press, 1977.

Smitherman, Geneva. *Talkin and Testifyin: The Language of Black America.* Boston: Houghton Mifflin, 1977.

Walker, Alice. *In Search of our Mothers' Gardens.* New York: Harcourt Brace, 1983.

SHIRLEY J. (S. J.) CORDELL-ROBINSON

The Black Woman: A Focus on "Strength of Character" in I Know Why the Caged Bird Sings

It has been said that a black woman has two strikes against her—being a woman and being born black. Alice Childress in an article in *Freedomways* (Volume 6, Number 1, Winter 1966) gives substance to this remark when she says that "the American Negro woman has been *particularly* and deliberately oppressed, in slavery and up to and including the present moment, above and beyond the general knowledge of the American citizen." Mary Helen Washington further states ("Black Women Image Makers," *Black World*, August, 1974) that "in approaching the question of the Black woman's image in the media and in literature, one's first impulse is to carefully scrutinize those negative and false depictions of the Black woman . . . [we] are all so familiar with—the tragic mulatto, the hot-blooded exotic whore, the strong black mammy. . . ."

It is not difficult then to surmise that the black woman has experienced and continues to experience character portrayal in literature and the media as sexual or matriarchal stereotypes, void of femininity, domineering, and lacking humaneness. To combat these pervasive depictions, numerous black authors, particularly the more contemporary, have worked to examine and eradicate the stereotyping of black women. Washington in the aforementioned article supports this contention by an implied prediction that writers like Alice Walker, Gwendolyn Brooks, Paule Marshall, Toni Morrison, Ann

Virginia English Bulletin, Volume 36, Number 2 (Winter 1986): pp. 36–39. © 1986 Shirley J. (S. J.) Cordell-Robinson.

Petry, Maya Angelou, and others have portrayed in their works "images of the Black woman so powerful and realistic that they can combat whatever stereotypes of Black women that still persist."

One notable technique to channel positive image projection of black women is through realistic characterization. This technique is attained in one of the most effective selections by and about black women, *I Know Why the Caged Bird Sings* by Maya Angelou.

Numerous critics collectively hail this work as not only a use of language, but also containing character portrayals of great strength and human dimension. What Angelou does is to elevate the image of herself and the black women in her life by telling her story using episodic details to illuminate personal and historical identity as well as give shape and meaning to the experiences from which that identity has evolved. Angelou's reality becomes the reality for many. Her "quest after self-acceptance," as one critic termed it, is the story line in the first of her series of autobiographical endeavors.

Maya Angelou's story begins with a journey. Her brother Bailey and she are traveling cross-country from California to Arkansas to live with their grandmother, a central figure who is to teach Maya perhaps the greatest lesson, that of character strength. "Momma" welcomes these three- and four-year-olds, and during the next five years, she attunes them to Southern living for blacks.

From Stamps, Arkansas, Maya and Bailey are taken back to St. Louis, Missouri, to live with their mother's family. This life-style is very different from the previous one. Living is fast paced, and mother, grandmother, aunts, and uncles are the kind that exude family closeness and a sense of protection. It is in St. Louis, however, that Maya experiences the greatest degradation that any person can: she is raped by her mother's boyfriend, and for a child of eight, the results are confusing as well as frightening.

From St. Louis, Maya and her brother are sent back to their grandmother's in Stamps and remain there until she is thirteen. Maya's existence is lifeless (she refers to it as "an old biscuit, dirty and inedible") until she meets Mrs. Bertha Flowers who was deemed "the aristocrat of black Stamps." Maya says that this woman threw her her first life line. Maya's love of reading begins early, having read Shakespeare and others at six, but Mrs. Flowers nurtures this love of reading and channels Maya to realms that even Momma found difficult to penetrate.

One of Maya's strongest moments of self-realization occurs while she is working for a white woman. Black children, and adults as well, are supposed to know "their place" in Stamps; but through a quiet emergence, Maya has assumed (by actions and reactions of her grandmother) the kind of subtlety she needed to rise above any feeling of inadequacy. The white woman continually refuses to call Maya's name correctly. During her tenure of work, Maya resolves the problem with Mrs. Cullinan. At Bailey's suggestion, she purposely breaks the woman's "Virginia China." When Mrs. Cullinan confronts Maya, she lashes out in anger because she has been accurately accused.

Later in the story, Maya experiences normal adolescent involvement. She finds a best friend, and she has her first crush. There are also sporadic remembrances of her molestation, but she is able to rechannel the negative implications. Maya launches herself into her schooling and graduates at twelve at the top of her eighth grade class. During the graduation ceremonies, Maya is able to put her heritage in perspective after an uninvited white official addresses the audience and relegates the lives of blacks in Stamps to aspirations such as maids, farmers, and other manservants. She has learned to be competitive, and this attitude will follow her to California and later enable her to vie for a position as a trolley car driver—the first black on the San Francisco streetcars.

The remaining sojourn of Maya includes her return to the West Coast where she lives with both parents, attends school, and shares in many experiences. One person, in particular, impresses Maya. Miss Kirwin, one of Maya's teachers, encourages her intellect and whets her dramatic appetites.

The story line is one of the book's major strengths, but Maya's understanding of certain characters' roles in her life is as true to the nurturing of children today as it was then: "The allegiances I owed at this time in my life would have made very strange bedfellows: Momma with her solemn determination . . . my mother and her gaiety, Miss Kirwin and her information. . . ."

Momma's strength as Maya perceives it is based on fantasy, but the dream will be tested in Chapter 24. The fantasy Maya envisions is needed to create a mechanism that will allow her to cope with racism. Maya has a painful toothache and Momma tries to convince the white dentist to pull the tooth. His response is what Maya needs to understand Momma's strength. "Annie, my policy is I'd rather stick my hand in a dog's mouth than in a nigger's." Maya fantasizes Momma's setting him straight and ordering him out of town by sundown. But as Momma explains it, she is aware of her powerlessness and she is cunning enough to wrangle $10 from the dentist to take Maya to the black dentist miles away. This kind of strength is antithetical to stereotypes of the matriarchal black woman.

Another character who influences Maya with her beauty and certainty is her mother Vivian Baxter. It may seem somewhat paradoxical that Maya can love and admire the mother who sent her to live with her grandmother. An examination of Vivian's characterization in the book reveals that Maya respected her mother's enthusiasm for life. The fact that she does not rear her children and that she lives her life socializing does not diminish her love for her children. As in the lives of others, some women simply cannot rear children, and they may or may not admit to this characteristic. Vivian clearly has an unusual understanding of herself.

Maya learns from the women in her life, and her quest of self-realization is only begun in *I Know Why the Caged Bird Sings*. She comes to grips with the beauty of her existence, not in terms of physical attributes, but in terms of love and loyalty to herself and to the other persons who helped to give meaning to her life.

In examining book reviews and critical evaluations, I found evaluators and critics to be more than generous in their praise of this work. They attest to Angelou's ability as a skillful writer because of the power of her images and the richness of the language. George E. Kent in *Phylon* (June, 1975) states that "Maya excels in portraits. No character becomes less than a well-etched type...."

When a work such as *Caged Bird* is reprinted innumerable times, the literary merit of it should be clear to most. However, some may find Maya's work objectionable, mainly because of the explicit descriptions during the period Maya experiences physical abuse. The language, too, may border on vulgarity for some. These aspects may have to be considered by teachers since use of the book with students may be met with opposition. If such opposition should occur, the fact that overt child abuse continues to be rampant in our society should be reason enough to defend the book. Maya's revelation of this most abhorrent act is not dwelled upon unnecessarily, and it is used to give her strong human dimensions. She never hates Mr. Freeman. Indeed, she seems to have forgiven him in the innocence she regained. She goes on with her life because there were people who supported her and helped her to find that strength that makes her the outstanding writer she has become.

CAROL E. NEUBAUER

An Interview with Maya Angelou

NEUBAUER: I see autobiography in general as a way for a writer to go back to her past and try to present what is left in memory but also to recover what has been lost through imagination and invention.

ANGELOU: Autobiography is for me a beloved which, like all beloveds, one is not given by family. One happens upon. You know, you turn the corner to the left instead of to the right. Stop in the parking lot and meet a beloved, or someone who becomes a beloved. And by the time I was half finished with *Caged Bird* I knew I loved the form—that I wanted to try to see what I could do with the form. Strangely enough, not as a cathartic force, not really; at any rate I never thought that really I was interested or am interested in autobiography for its recuperative power. I liked the form—the literary form—and by the time I started *Gather Together* I had gone back and reread Frederick Douglass' slave narrative. Anyway, I love the idea of the slave narrative, using the first person singular, really meaning always the third person plural. I love that. And I see it all the time in the black literature, in the blues and spirituals and the poetry, in essays James Baldwin uses it. But I've tried in each book to let the new voice come through and that's what makes it very difficult for me not to impose the voice of 1980 onto the voice I'm writing from 1950, possibly.

The Massachusetts Review, Volume 28 (Summer 1987): pp. 286–292. © 1987 The Massachusetts Review.

NEUBAUER: And so when you say you look for a new voice you don't mean the voice of the present or the time of writing the autobiographical account, but rather of that period of your past. That must be difficult.

ANGELOU: Very. Very difficult, but I think that in writing autobiography that that's what is necessary to really move it from almost an "as told to" to an "as remembered" state. And really for it to be a creative and artistic literary art form. I believe I came close to recreating the voice in *Gather Together* of that young girl—eratic, sporadic, fractured. I think in each case I've come close. Rather a sassy person in *Singin' and Swingin'*.

NEUBAUER: It seemed that in *The Heart of a Woman,* either the voice was more complex or else there was more than one voice at work. There seemed to be the voice of that time in your life and yet another voice commenting on that time.

ANGELOU: It seems so, but I looked at that quite carefully and at the period I think it is the voice because I was really coming into a security about who I was and what I was about, but the security lasted sometimes for three or four days or maybe through a love affair or into a love affair or into a job. I think it would be like smoke in a room. It would just dissipate and I would suddenly be edgewalking again. I would be one of those children in the rye, playing very perilously close to the precipice and aware of it. I tried very hard for the voice. I remember the woman very well.

NEUBAUER: What I saw in *Heart of a Woman* was not so much that there were two voices talking against one another, but rather that a voice from a more recent time commented ironically on the predominant voice of that time in the past. The irony of you as the writer and the autobiographical presence coming through.

ANGELOU: It is really one of the most difficult. First, well, I don't know what comes first in that case. Whether it is the insistence to write well while trying to speak in a voice thirty years ago. I'm now writing a new book and trying to speak in that voice—the voice of 1963 and what I know about writing in 1984. It really is difficult.

NEUBAUER: Does it become more difficult the closer you get to the present?

ANGELOU: Yes, absolutely. Because by '63 my command of English was *almost* what it is today and I had been very much influenced by Vus Make. He had really influenced my thinking, and his English was exquisite. My reading in other languages also by that time had very much influenced my speaking and I was concerned about eloquence by 1960. So this book is really the most difficult and I've been ducking and dodging it too. I know this morning I should call my editor and tell him I have not forgotten him. He's very much on my mind and the work is very much on my mind. I don't know what I'm going to do when I finish this book. I *may* try to go back and pick up some of the incidents that I left out of maybe *Caged Bird* or *Gather Together* or any of the books. I don't know how to do that.

NEUBAUER: Are you thinking of autobiography?

ANGELOU: Yes.

NEUBAUER: That's fascinating. One of the things I'm interested in particularly is how the present influences the autobiographical past. I think what you're engaged in doing now and have been since *Caged Bird* is something that's never been done before in this scope. Each volume of yours is a whole and has a unity that works for that volume alone. If you were to go back to the period of *Caged Bird* that would add another wrinkle in this question of time and different voices.

ANGELOU: I don't know how I will do it, and I don't know if I'll be able to do it. But I think there are facets. When I look at a stained glass window, it's very much like this book. I have an idea that the books are very much like the Everyman stories so that there is greed and kindness and generosity and cruelty, oppression, and sloth. And I think of the period I'm going to write about and I try to see which of the incidents in which greed, say it's green, which of these that happened to me during that period will most demonstrate that particular condition. Now some are more rich, but I refuse them. I do not select them because it's very hard to write drama without falling into melodrama. So the incidents I reject, I find myself unable to write about without becoming melodramatic. I just can't see how to write it. In *Gather Together* there is an incident in which a man almost killed me—tried to, in fact—and kept me for three days and he was a mad man, literally. My escape was so incredible, literally incredible, that there was no way to write it, absolutely, to make it credible and not melodramatic.

NEUBAUER: Have you ever chosen to take another incident in that case, perhaps one that might not have even happened, and use that as a substitute?

ANGELOU: No, because there are others which worked, which did happen, and which showed either cruelty or the irony of escape. So was able to write that rather than the other.

NEUBAUER: I see. So you didn't have to sacrifice the core of the experience.

ANGELOU: No, I never sacrificed. It's just choosing which of those greens or which of those reds to make that kind of feeling.

NEUBAUER: It's a beautiful metaphor, the greens, the reds and the light coming through the window. Because in a sense, memory works that way; it filters out past work. And yet an autobiographer has a double task—at least double, probably triple or quadruple—in some ways the filtering has been done beyond your control on an unconscious level. But as a writer working in the present you, too, are making selections or choices, which complicate the experience.

ANGELOU: There is so much to talk to you about on this subject. I have, I think, due to all those years of not talking, which again, I chose to minimize in *Caged Bird* because it's hard to write that without, again, the melodramas leaking in. But because of those years of muteness, I think my memory was developed in queer ways, because I remember—I have total recall—or I have none at all. None. And there is no pattern to the memory, so that I would forget all the good and the bad of a certain time, or I will remember *only* the bad of a certain time, or I will remember *only* the good. But when I remember it, I will remember *everything* about it. *Everything.* The outside noises, the odors in the room, the way my clothes were feeling—everything. I just have it, or I remember nothing. I am sure that is a part of the sort of psychological problems I was having and how the memory went about its business knitting itself.

NEUBAUER: Almost as a treasure chest or a defense.

ANGELOU: Yes, both, I guess. But in a sense, not really a defense, because some of the marvelous things I've not remembered. For instance, one of the promises I've exacted from every lover or husband who promised to be a permanent fixture was that *if* I die in the house, if something happened, get me outside. Please don't let me die in the room, or open the window and let me see some rolling hills. Let me see, please. Now, my memory of Stamps, Arkansas, is flat, dirt, the trees around the pond. But everything just flat and mean. When I agreed to go to join Bill Moyers for his creativity program, I flew to Dallas and decided to drive to Stamps because I wanted to sneak up on Stamps. It's, I guess, 200 miles or more. When I drove out of Texas into Arkansas, Stamps is 30 miles from Texas. I began to see the undulating hills. I couldn't believe it! I couldn't believe it! It's beautiful! It's what I love. But the memory had completely gone.

NEUBAUER: When you're working, for example, on your present book, are there things that help you remember that period or any period in the past better?

ANGELOU: Well, a curious thing has happened to me with every book. When I start to work—start to plan it—I encounter people whom I have known in that time, which is really queer. I've wondered if I would encounter them anyway, or if it's a case of "when the student is ready the teacher appears." If I simply wouldn't see their value if I would encounter them and wouldn't see their value for what I'm working on, because I wouldn't be working on that. That is one of the very interesting things. I'm working on Ghana now and this summer I went to London to write a play. I saw a sister friend there from Ghana and suddenly about fifteen Ghanaians; soon I was speaking Fanti again and they were reminding me, "Do you remember that time when?" and suddenly it all came right up my nostrils. But what I do is just pull myself away from everything and everybody and then begin the most frightening of the work. And that is going back. I'm always afraid I'll never come out. Every morning I wake up, usually about 5:30 and try to get to my work room. I keep a little room in a hotel. Nothing on the walls, nothing belonging to me, nothing. I go in and I try to be in by 6:30 and try to get back, get back. Always, for the first half hour is spent wondering if anybody cares for me enough to come and pull me out. Suppose I can't get out?

NEUBAUER: That's a difficult road to retrace—to find.

ANGELOU: Like an enchanted . . . I know that sounds romantic, but you know how I mean. But I do get back and I remember one thing and I think, "Yes, and what are the other things like that that happened?" And maybe a second one will come. It's all there. *All of it* is there.

NEUBAUER: Even down to the finest details and the dialogues, what you said to the people you were with.

ANGELOU: The sound of the voices. And I write wurrrrrrrrrrrrrr.

NEUBAUER: How long do you write if you go in at 6:30?

ANGELOU: Well, I'm out by 12:30, unless it's really happening. If it's really happening I'll stay till 2:00, but no longer. No longer. And then get out and go home and shower and make a lovely lunch and drink a lot of wine and try to come down. Get back. Stop in a shop, "Hi, how are you? Fine. . . ." So I can ascertain that I do live and people remember me.

NEUBAUER: Do you leave it in the middle of an incident so that you have a way back, or do you write to the end of each one?

ANGELOU: No, I can't write to the end of the incident. I will write to a place that's safe. Nothing will leak away now; I've got it. Then at night I'll read it and try to edit it.

NEUBAUER: The same night?

ANGELOU: The same night. Try to edit it for writing, a little of it. And then begin again the next day. Lordy.

NEUBAUER: Is it a frightening journey because of the deep roots from that time to the present? Do you feel a kind of vulnerability?

ANGELOU: I am not afraid of the ties. I cherish them, rather. It's the vulnerability. It's like using drugs or something. It's allowing oneself to be hypnotized. That's frightening, because then we have no defenses, nothing. We've slipped down the well and every side is slippery. And how on earth are you going to come out? That's scary. But I've chosen it, and I've chosen this mode as my mode.

NEUBAUER: How far will the fifth volume go?

ANGELOU: Actually, it's a new kind. It's really quite a new voice. I'm looking at the black American resident, me and the other black American residents in Ghana, and trying to see all the magic of the eternal quest of human beings to go home again. That is maybe what life is anyway. To return to the Creator. All of that naiveté, the innocence of trying to. That awful rowing towards God, whatever it is. Whether it's to return to your village or the lover you lost or the youth that some people want to return to or the beauty that some want to return to.

NEUBAUER: Writing autobiography frequently involves this quest to return to the past, to the home. Sometimes, if the home can't be found, if it can't be located again, then that home or that love or that family, whatever has been lost, is recreated or invented.

ANGELOU: Yes, of course. That's it! That's what I'm seeing in this trek back to Africa. That in so many cases that idealized home of course is nonexistent. In so many cases some black Americans created it on the spot. On the spot. And I did too. Created something, looked, seemed like what we have idealized very far from reality. It's going to be a painful, hard book to write, in that not only all I the stuff that it cost me to write it, but there will be a number of people who will be disappointed. So I have to deal with that once the book is out. The main thing is getting it out.

NEUBAUER: Are their opinions becoming more and more of a consideration as you move closer to the present in your autobiographies?

ANGELOU: Yes, indeed, because in some cases I can't use names. When I use names I have to get permission from people who are alive. I called Vus Make just when I was about half way through *Heart of a Woman* and I told him. He lives in Darsalan now. And I said I'm writing a book in the time which you featured. So he said, "I will sign any permission. I will give any rights to you, for I know you will not lie. However, I am sure I shall disagree with your interpretation of the truth."

NEUBAUER: I know I speak for many in saying how much I am looking forward to your next book or your next "interpretation of the truth."

JOANNE MEGNA-WALLACE

Simone de Beauvoir and Maya Angelou: Birds of a Feather

Simone de Beauvoir and Maya Angelou appear to have little in common. Beauvoir is French, Angelou American; Beauvoir is white, Angelou black; Beauvoir lived most of her life in the city of Paris, while Angelou's childhood was primarily spent in the rural town of Stamps, Arkansas. But despite these circumstantial differences, both women chose to write their life stories, stories which describe remarkably parallel evolutions from conventional, dutiful daughters to autonomous individuals.

In this paper, I will explore and compare the first volume of each author's autobiography, Beauvoir's *Memoirs of a Dutiful Daughter,* and Angelou's *I Know Why the Caged Bird Sings.* Both authors continue their personal accounts in succeeding volumes, but it is the years of childhood and adolescence which reveal the most about their psychological development and achievement of independence that will be the focus of this study. Their autobiographies will be analyzed in light of feminist psychoanalytic and sociological perspectives, drawing on the work of Carol Gilligan and Nancy Chodorow as well as the recent critical work on women's autobiography by Sidonie Smith.

Both Beauvoir's and Angelou's early childhood years are characterized by deep love and respect for a mother figure which provides stability, and a strong sense of self and self-worth in the case of Beauvoir. Beauvoir credits the family's maid with her "feeling of unalterable security,"[1] and tells us that

Simone de Beauvoir Studies, Volume 6 (1989): pp. 49–55. © 1989 Simone de Beauvior Society.

her mother inspired in her "the tenderest feelings." (*MDD*, 6) Beauvoir greatly feared her mother's disapproval, her "black look," (*MDD*, 6) and although
she occasionally raged against orders and prohibitions she perceived as arbi-
trary, she writes, "I never seriously called authority in question. . . . I accepted
without question the values and the tenets of those around me." (*MDD*, 14)

Angelou was born Marguerite Johnson, and initially her childhood was
less stable than Beauvoir's. Her parents divorced when she was three years old
and she and her older brother Bailey were sent to Arkansas to live with her
paternal grandmother, whom she called "Momma." Momma was strict and
devoutly religious, and although Maya admits that she was often baffled by
adult behavior and beliefs, she clearly loved and respected her grandmother.
About Momma, Angelou writes, "I don't think she ever knew that a deep-
brooding love hung over everything she touched."[2] When Maya was told that
Momma used to be pretty, she recalls, "I saw only her power and strength."
(*CB*, 38) This substitute mother-daughter relationship (and her deep feelings
for her brother Bailey) provided some security to Maya, an otherwise lonely
and alienated child. The opening lines of her story, taken from a poem, are
testimony to her early sense of displacement: "What you looking at me for? I
didn't come to stay . . ." (*CB*, 1)

Sidonie Smith, in her article entitled "The Song of a Caged Bird: Maya
Angelou's Quest after Self-Acceptance," notes that the rejection of Bailey
and Maya by their parents is " . . . internalize[d] and translate[d] as a rejection of self: ultimately the loss of home occasions the loss of self-worth."[3] In
addition, Maya's sensitivity to the racism which permeated her environment
further contributed to her sense of inferiority. But Smith acknowledges the
positive impact of Angelou's relationship with her grandmother in her quest
for self-acceptance: " . . . although she is lonely, although she suffers from her
feelings of ugliness and abandonment, the strength of Momma's arms contains some of that loneliness."[4]

Recent feminist studies emphasize the importance of the mother-
daughter relationship for woman's psychological development. Both Beauvoir
and Angelou give prominence to the role of the mother figure, and their narrative strategies bear witness to the impact of this relationship on them, and
ultimately on their writing. For what is striking about their narrative choices
is that they do not only write their own lives, they describe in detail the role
others have played in shaping their identities and destinies. Nancy Chodorow
maintains that "Because of their mothering by women, girls come to experience themselves as less separate than boys, as having more permeable ego
boundaries. Girls come to define themselves more in relation to others."[5]

Thus far we have seen the importance of the maternal other for Angelou
and Beauvoir. Each also acknowledges the significant role played by her sibling
in her childhood. About her sister Hélène, called Poupette, Beauvoir writes,

"She was my liegeman, my *alter ego,* my double; we could not do without one another." (*MDD,* 42.) Later she adds, "I owe a great debt to my sister for helping me to externalize many of my dreams in play: she also helped me to save my daily life from silence; through her I got into the habit of wanting to communicate with people." (*MDD,* 44.) Beauvoir describes the lasting bond that developed between the sisters as she taught Hélène to read, write, and count, and concludes, "Thanks to my sister I was asserting my right to personal freedom; she was my accomplice, my subject, my creature." (*MDD,* 45.)

Similarly, Angelou writes about her brother: "Bailey was the greatest person in my world. And the fact that he was my brother, my only brother, and I had no sisters to share him with, was such good fortune that it made me want to live a Christian life just to show God that I was grateful." (*CB,* 17.) She concludes her introduction to her brother with the words "Of all the needs ... a lonely child has, the one that must be satisfied, if there is going to be hope and a hope of wholeness, is the unshaking need for an unshakable God. My pretty black brother was my Kingdom Come." (*CB,* 19.) Thus each author expresses gratitude for her sibling and credits this "other" with helping her to achieve what she will come to value most: for Angelou, it is wholeness; for Beauvoir, personal freedom and an ability to communicate with others.

As Beauvoir and Angelou grew older, they naturally had more interaction outside their families and each found a "best friend." Around age ten, Beauvoir met Elizabeth Mabille, called Zaza. Zaza is a constant presence throughout the first volume of her memoirs, and it has even been argued that the dutiful daughter of the title is as much Zaza as it is Simone.[6] Beauvoir was attracted to Zaza's naturalness and spontaneity: "We would talk about our school work, our reading, our common friends, our teachers, and about what we knew of the world ... " (*MDD,* 93.) She concludes Part I of the memoirs with the admission, "I could think of nothing better in the world than being myself, and loving Zaza." (*MDD,* 96.)

It is also at age ten that Maya Angelou met Louise Kendricks. After a good giggle over an impromptu game of looking into the sky and trying to fall into it, they became friends. According to Angelou, "My friendship with Louise was solidified over jacks, hopscotch, and confessions, deep and dark, exchanged often after many a 'Cross your heart you won't tell?' (*CB,* 133.) These descriptions of friendship are consistent with the observations of Carol Gilligan in her well-known work *In a Different Voice.* According to Gilligan and the study by Janet Lever she cites, "... girls' play tends to occur in smaller, more intimate groups, often the best-friend dyad, and in private places.... it points less ... toward learning to take the role of 'the generalized other,' less toward the abstraction of human relationships. But it fosters the development of the empathy and sensitivity necessary for taking the role of 'the particular other'...."[7]

Throughout this study, we have seen how each author valorizes the "particular other" in her own life story. The role of another is again underscored as each describes the mentors she credits with her intellectual development. The lectures of Robert Garric, professor of French literature at the Institut Sainte-Marie, opened up new horizons for Beauvoir. Through him she came to believe that she had to overcome class differences and dedicate her life to serving humanity through her writing. And later there was Sartre, whom Beauvoir met while preparing for the competitive teaching exam, the agrégation. About their study sessions, she writes, ". . . it was always he who knew most about all the authors and all the aspects of our syllabus: we merely listened to him talking. . . . he used to do his utmost to help us to benefit from his knowledge. . . . I was staggered by his generosity." (*MDD*, 335) Beauvoir sums up the importance of this relationship with the words, "Sartre corresponded exactly to the dream-companion I had longed for since I was fifteen." (*MDD*, 345)

For Maya Angelou, it was a woman who provided spiritual and intellectual guidance. Upon her return from a year-long stay with her real mother in St. Louis, where at thirteen she was the victim of sexual abuse, Angelou was invited to the home of Mrs. Bertha Flowers, "the aristocrat of Black Stamps." (*CB*, 77) About her, Angelou writes, "When she chose to smile on me, I always wanted to thank her . . . She was one of the few gentlewomen I have ever known, and has remained throughout my life the measure of what a human being can be." (*CB*, 78) Mrs. Flowers taught Maya tolerance for others, love for books, and, most importantly, self-esteem. Angelou remarks, "I was liked, and what a difference it made. I was respected not as Mrs. Henderson's grandchild or Bailey's sister but for just being Marguerite Johnson." (*CB*, 85)

Repeatedly, Beauvoir and Angelou express gratitude for the presence of "particular others" in their lives and give credit to them for the persons they have become. In light of the observations of Nancy Chodorow and Carol Gilligan on the psychosexual and social development of young girls, we see that the femaleness of these two authors helps to explain this orientation toward others.

Despite their attachment and gratitude to others, however, both Beauvoir and Angelou eventually perceived the circumstances of their lives as a cage and found that they needed to break away from family authority figures and free themselves from stifling social conventions in order to achieve autonomy. Beauvoir chronicles the stormy relationship with her parents, especially her mother, during her adolescence. Although she believed that rejection of her parents' bourgeois values would bring her only loneliness and alienation, she recognized that "In order to understand the world and find myself I had to save myself from them." (*MDD*, 194) For Angelou, a move to San Francisco during World War II to live with her mother was the first in a series of incidents which signaled a profound change in her sense of self. About San Francisco, she observed, "The air of collective displacement, the impermanence of life in wartime . . . tended to dissipate my own sense of not belonging." (*CB*, 179) Later, while visiting her father, Angelou was stabbed by his jealous girlfriend and spent the next month living in a junkyard with an assortment of other homeless children. Her recounting of this episode concludes with the words, "The unquestioning acceptance by my peers had dislodged the familiar insecurity. . . . I was never again to sense myself so solidly outside the pale of the human race." (*CB*, 216) Angelou eventually applied for a job on the San Francisco streetcars and, despite repeated rejection, finally became the first black person hired as a conductorette.

At the conclusion of these autobiographies, Zaza has died and Angelou has just given birth to a baby boy. Beauvoir is guilt-ridden because she herself had escaped "the revolting fate that had lain ahead of us," (*MDD*, 360) while Zaza had fallen victim to the tyranny of bourgeois values and practices. Angelou is so in awe of her newborn son that she is afraid to touch him until her mother insists that the baby spend the night sleeping next to its mother. She wakes up to find that she has instinctively protected her baby, not rolled over on him as she had feared.

The wheel, then, has come full circle. Having achieved a certain degree of independence through their intelligence and strength, the care and concern of both authors returns to others. And this is nowhere more evident than in their stated reasons for writing their autobiographies. They offer themselves as examples to others, to inspire and to teach. Beauvoir declares that she wrote *Memoirs of a Dutiful Daughter* in order to pay a debt to Zaza, while Angelou hoped her work would serve as an example to young people of her belief that "You may encounter many defeats, but you must not be defeated."[8]

The question remains, "Is the intersubjective pattern adopted by Beauvoir and Angelou unique to them?" Sidonie Smith, in her work entitled *A Poetics of Women's Autobiography,* reviews the various theories of women's autobiography to date and cites among them "theories that distinguish women's autobiographies by the way in which women seem to unfold their story through their relationship to a significant 'other'. . . ."[9] Smith acknowledges, "It may be that, as theorists of language and literature suggest, woman's subjectivity and therefore her text unfold narratively in patterns tied to her different psychosexual development."[10] She also wonders whether attention to the other is "a culturally conditioned manifestation" and whether all autobiographies do not proceed "by means of a self/other intersubjectivity and intertextuality."[11] Smith does not answer these questions, nor can I claim to give definitive answers, but I suspect that if a thorough study of male and female autobiographies were done, one would find that interpersonal factors are a more integral part of women's autobiographies than men's. Further, I would agree with those theorists Smith cites who tie these intersubjective narrative patterns to woman's psychosexual development. These challenges suggest the need for further inquiry. Consistent with a practice which has also come to be considered female, I will leave you, I hope, with a sense of an opening rather than closure.

Notes

1. Simone de Beauvoir, *Memoirs of a Dutiful Daughter.* Trans. James Kirkus (New York: Harper and Row, 1959), p. 5. Further quotations from this source will be cited in the text as *MDD*.

2. Maya Angelou, *I Know Why the Caged Bird Sings.* (New York: Random House, 1969), p. 47. Further quotations from this source will be cited in the text as *CB*.

3. Sidonie Smith, "The Song of a Caged Bird: Maya Angelou's Quest after Self-Acceptance," *The Southern Humanities Review* (Fall 1973), pp. 365–375. repr. Dedria Bryfonski, ed., *Contemporary Literary Criticism* 12 (Detroit: Gale Research Co., 1980), p. 10.,

4. Smith, p. 10

5. Nancy Chodorow, *The Reproduction of Mothering* (Berkeley: University of California Press, 1978), p. 93.

6. See Catherine Portuges, "Attachment and Separation in *The Memoirs of a Dutiful Daughter,*" *Yale French Studies,* 72 (1986), p. 109.

7. Carol Gilligan, *In a Different Voice.* (Cambridge: Harvard University Press, 1982), p. 11.

8. Bryfonski, *Contemporary Literary Criticism,* p. 9.

9. Sidonie Smith, *A Poetics of Women's Autobiography.* (Bloomington: Indiana University Press, 1987), p. 18.

10. Ibid., p. 13.

11. Ibid., p. 18.

ELIZABETH FOX-GENOVESE

Myth and History: Discourse of Origins in Zora Neale Hurston and Maya Angelou

*D*ust *Tracks on a Road*. It does not take much imagination to glimpse the traces of the South in Zora Neale Hurston's title. Roads on which feet leave dust tracks are dusty roads—hot, sun-baked, dirt roads that comb the Southern heartland from South Carolina to Texas. Dusty roads link Eaton-ville, Florida, to Stamps, Arkansas. These are the roads that bare-footed black Southern women have traveled since slavery days. These are the roads that cheaply shod black Southern women still travel on foot, or on dilapi-dated buses. Trains now link these Southern towns, if not to each other, to the rest of the country. But the roads remain, like a faded tracing on the face of the South. The roads of black folks delineate the topography of those centuries of oppression which emancipation could not eradicate. The roads of black folks, like a grid of veins and arteries, join disparate communities and scattered women in the throbbing center of a common past.

I Know Why the Caged Bird Sings. The fracturing of slavery's shackles formally freed individuals, but left blacks as a people caged. Unbreakable bars closed black communities in upon themselves, denying both the communi-ties and the individuals who composed them access to the surrounding white world. Within those cages, black communities developed their own vibrant life, black women raised up black girls in the way that they should go. Sing-ing in the face of danger, singing to thwart the stings of insolence, singing

Black American Literature Forum, Volume 24, Number 2 (Summer 1990): pp. 221–235. © 1990 Estate of Elizabeth Fox-Genovese.

to celebrate their Lord, singing to testify to a better future, singing with the life blood of their people, black women defied their imprisonment. The cages constrained, but did not stifle them. The songs of confinement grounded the vitality of their tradition, launched the occasional fledgling to freedom.

The collective identity of African-American women sinks its roots in the roads and fields, the towns and villages of the South. In the pages of white Southern women, the South frequently figures as a natural wonder. For them, towering oaks, dusky cypresses, resplendent magnolias embody the splendor of their region—its distinct physical presence.[1] For black women, that landscape wears a more ominous face, for its splendors belong to the whites. For black women, the South wears a human face, with the face of danger always shadowing the face of love. Above all, however conflictedly, the South remains home—the wellspring of self.

Slavery days are long gone, but their traces linger, shooting up like those uncontrollable weeds that can eat up a garden in the course of a summer. Even during slavery, free black communities flourished in the North and in pockets of the South. But the very name "free black" belies those communities' freedom from the heavy hand of slavery as a social system and indexes their ties to the South. The tradition of African-American autobiography began, in William L. Andrews's phrase, as the determination "to tell a free story."[2] The obsession with freedom betokened the indissoluble, if submerged, obsession with slavery. Race grounded the association. In a country in which only black people were enslaved, blackness and unfreedom merged in a shadowy negation of the virtues of freedom. Slavery grounded and guaranteed racism. Slavery confirmed the association between freedom and virtue, between freedom and whiteness, between whiteness and virtue. Slavery negated the individualism of blacks singly, negated the autonomy of blacks as a community. And these very negations ineluctably bound "free" blacks to the history of their enslaved brothers and sisters. In dissociating themselves from the condition of their enslaved people, they risked dissociating themselves from their people—from their race.

In the roads and cages of the South, during slavery times as thereafter, lay the history—the pre-history—of each and every black self. These roads and cages embodied the specific history that made the black self a singular self, rather than an accidental exemplar of some archetypical self. Only through recuperation of that history could African-American men and women represent their discrete selves as whole and free. The challenge of representing a metaphysically free yet historically specific self proved daunting, although never insurmountable.[3] And if daunting for black men, how much more so for black women? For if black men confronted the specific challenge of demonstrating their manhood in a culture that viewed enslavement as the negation not only of freedom but of manly virtue, black women remained torn between demonstrating their virtuous womanhood and their individualism. The pressures to opt for the demonstration of true womanhood were strong. Many black men accepted the values of white society that held that a dependent and subservient woman offered stellar proof of a man's manhood. Many white women expected black women faithfully to adhere to white culture's images of true womanhood as retiring and self-abnegating. But professed dependence and self-denial threw black women back into the arms of slavery, even if now in the service of their own people.

Gender, race, and condition wove a tight web around black women's possibilities for self-representation, especially since for them, as for their men, any understanding of the self led back over dusty roads to Southern cages.[4] Worse, the conventions of womanhood that whites had developed and middle-class blacks apparently embraced branded the very act of authorship as pushy and unfeminine. As women and as blacks, African-American women autobiographers were, in some measure, bound to construct their self-representations through available discourses, and in interaction with intended readers. For them, as for white women and for white and black men, the self had to be represented in the (recognizable) discourses of one or more interpretive communities. To be sure, their self-representations could variously—and even simultaneously—comply with, subvert, or transform prevailing discourses. But the abiding danger persisted of seeing themselves through the prism of a (white) andocentric discourse, literally through men's eyes, through white eyes.

At the beginning of the twentieth century, American culture knew no black discourse of Southern roads and cages. The discourses existed, but did not figure prominently—and certainly not independently—in the dominant discourses of the country. Here and there a bit of dialect would surface, here and there a trace of song, but almost always through the objectifying consciousness of a white observer. The music, the tales, the speech of black communities remained largely confined to the Southern oral culture in which it flowered.[5] *In Caged Bird,* Maya Angelou recalls the double language of her teens:

> My education and that of my Black associates were quite different from the education of our white schoolmates. In the classroom we all learned past participles, but in the streets and in our homes the Blacks learned to drop s's from plurals and suffixes from past-tense verbs. We were alert to the gap separating the written word from the colloquial. We learned to slide out of one language and into another without being conscious of the effort. At school, in a given situation, we might respond with "That's not unusual." But in the street, meeting the same situation, we easily said, "It be's like that sometimes" (219).

It required education in the dominant (white) speech for her to recognize the black language of the streets, and beyond it the language of Stamps, as distinct. Without immersion in white culture, she would never have recognized the distinctiveness of the speech of her people, would simply have accepted it as a given. Similarly, Hurston remembered the chinaberry blossoms of Eatonville and that, as a child, she had "loved the fleshy, white fragrant blooms" but had not made too much of them. "They were too common in my neighborhood." But when she got to New York she "found out that the people called them gardenias, and that the flowers cost a dollar each" and was impressed (18). Black American speech has penetrated the dominant culture through the writings of literate blacks who have recuperated the oral culture of their people through the prism of that dominant culture, which has suggested new ways of seeing, writing, interpreting that culture. And, for African-American autobiographers in particular, the culture of their people has remained the seedbed of their origins as selves. But when they have written of that culture, they inescapably have written as exiles. Their very writing betokens the chasm that separates them from folk culture as oral culture.

In different ways, Zora Neale Hurston and Maya Angelou broke ground for new representations of the African-American female self. *Dust Tracks,* published in 1942, and *Caged Bird,* published in 1969, explicitly reclaim the Southern past as the grounding of their authors' identities. Both explicitly reject white norms of womanhood as models. In Hurston's pages, the Southern past reemerges as a mythic past suitable for the unique self; in Angelou's pages, it acquires a historical and sociological specificity that helps to account for the modern strength of the female self as survivor.

"Like the dead-seeming, cold rocks, I have memories within that came out of the material that went to make me. Time and place have had their say." Hurston thus opens *Dust Tracks* by explicitly reclaiming her concrete origins, by tying her memories to the permanence of cold rocks.[6] She was "born in a Negro town," not, she insists, "the black back-side of an average town." And she likens the town, Eatonville, Florida, to "hitting a straight lick with a crooked stick." Never in anyone's plans, the town was "a byproduct of something else. It all started with three white men on a ship off the coast of Brazil"(3). A tale of adventure, daring, and happenstances resulted, on August 18, 1886, in that Negro town's becoming "the first of its kind in America, and perhaps in the world" (10). And the spirit of those unique founders "has reached beyond the grave"—implicitly to Hurston herself. Hurston underscores the mythical origins by concluding the chapter, "It was in the late eighties that the stars fell, and many of the original settlers date their coming 'just before, or just after the stars fell'" (11). Thus the place that had its say in her origins was unlike any other the world has known, and the time was the time of falling stars.

In later days, Hurston's Mama "exhorted her children at every opportunity to 'jump at de sun'" (20–21). If they did not land there, they would at least "get off the ground." By then, her Papa "did not feel so hopeful. Let well enough alone. It did not do for Negroes to have too much spirit." And he always threatened "to break mine or kill me in the attempt," insisting that sooner or later Hurston would fall victim to white "posses with ropes and guns." But Mama, unruffled, merely responded "'Zora is my young'un'" and predicted that she would "'come out more than conquer'" (21). By which she meant, Hurston translates for her readers, that Zora's disposition was like her mother's, not her father's.

Hurston's discussion of her parents laces the star-falling magic of Eatonville with unmistakable traces of the harsh realities of black Southern life. Her father, reputedly the offspring of a white man, and thus possibly the offspring of a rape, conjures up in his wonderful looks the price that such a "buck" would have fetched under slavery. His "over-the-creek" origins temper his ambition, even in all-black Eatonville, with the fearsome knowledge of white folks' power. Uppityness, impudence, a tongue can only bring Zora retribution. And if talking back can wreak these horrors, what can be expected of writing back, or simply writing about? The will to aspire comes from her mother, that slip of a girl who had the imagination to defy her successful family by marrying the man who captured her fancy. Thus Hurston, like Angelou a generation later, links her own resolve to the grit and courage of Southern black women. But Hurston translates her mother's words for her literate readers.

Turning to her own birth, Hurston admits that her account "is all hearsay."[7] Her father, she muses, probably never "got over the trick he felt that I played on him by getting born a girl" (27), thus suggesting by her wording that her having been born a girl at all was an accident—that her femaleness is separable from her self, her "I." Such play on gender—and even race—as distinct from the essence of her self pervades the account. In describing her father's abiding disgust at her femaleness she remarks, "A little of my sugar used to sweeten his coffee right now." And then translates, "That is a Negro way of saying his patience was short with me" (27). She thus reminds her readers that she speaks white as well as "Negro" and thereby distances herself from the father who, she claims, had not wanted her. And turning the tables on him, Hurston replaces him at the scene of her birth with a "white man of many acres and things" who, knowing that her father was away, stopped by to bring her mother sweet potatoes and, seeing "how things were, and, being the kind of man he was, . . . took out his Barlow Knife and cut the navel cord" (29). Thus, on a mythically storming night, Zora came into the world "grannied" by a white man, who, in contrast to her father, proudly pronounced her a "God-damned fine baby." As she owed her birth, so did Zora owe her name, to an extraordinary intervention. Her mother had promised a friend, a Mrs. Neale, that she could name the baby if it were a girl. Mrs. Neale had picked Zora up somewhere and thought it very pretty. "Perhaps she had read it somewhere, or somebody back in those woods was smoking Turkish cigarettes" (30). From the start, Hurston suggests, that name brought her under the sign of literacy or exotic fantasy.

The play on identity pervades Hurston's account of her early life, which she depicts largely as the development of her "inside search." Time and again her ceaseless, searching questions ran up against the wall of old folks' impatience. The old folks—the black community—had been told how things were "and that had been enough for them, or to put it in Negro idiom, nobody didn't tell 'em, but they heard" (33). The collective wisdom of the oral culture did not satisfy Zora, who kept straining for something beyond the horizon. In particular, the young Zora yearned to "find out about the end of things. I had no doubts about the beginnings. They were somewhere in the five acres that was home to me. Most likely in Mama's room" (36–37).

Her father, who had opposed her birth, opposed her in her quests as well. He especially opposed her desire for a "'fine black riding horse with white leather saddle and bridles'" with which to ride to the horizon. In his outraged opinion, the mere desire for such a horse was "'a sin and a shame!'" Who did she think she was? She certainly was not like any of his other children. "'Lemme tell you something right now, my young lady; you ain't white.'" "That," Hurston annotates, "is a Negro saying that means 'Don't be too ambitious. You are a Negro and they are not meant to have but so much'" (38). But she did want a horse, and if she could not have one, she wanted nothing else. Since he would not give her one, she made one up: She would have her horse by her own efforts. So, implicitly, in her mind she would be white. Zora did not meet the expectations of her community much better than she met those of her father. "So I was driven inward. I lived an exciting life unseen" (40). The only person she pleased was the white man who had grannied her and who admiringly and affectionately enjoined her, "'Snidlits, don't be a nigger. . . . Niggers lie and lie!'" "The word Nigger," Hurston explains, "used in this sense does not mean race. It means a weak, contemptible person of any race" (41). Even as a child, she claims, she "knew without being told that he was not talking about my race when he advised me not to be a nigger. He was talking about class rather than race" (43). For, as he explained to her, people who lie are scared of something. She must never lie. "'Nothing can't lick you if you never get skeered'" (41). She had only to keep on fighting.

Zora's inner life received fresh material from school, which she loved, and, especially, from reading, which fed her imagination and disillusioned her with the world she knew. "My soul was with the gods and my body in the village. People just would not act like gods" (56). In this frame of mind, Zora experienced the twelve visions that mapped the stations of her future life and cut her off from her community. Longing to be like everybody else, she stood alone "in a world of vanished communion with my kind, which is worse than if it had never been. Nothing is so desolate as a place where life has been and gone" (59). And, Hurston intervenes, "I consider that my real childhood ended with the coming of the pronouncements" (60). Zora's visions were rapidly succeeded by the death of her mother, which in turn was succeeded by the beginnings of her wanderings. Zora's mother's death brought the early chapter of her life to a close: "Mama died at sundown and changed a world"; "that moment was the end of a phase in my life." Thenceforward, she was adrift. "That hour began my wanderings. Not so much in geography, but in time. Then not so much in time as in spirit" (89). Her adult journey is another story, although bits of it figure in the later chapters of *Dust Tracks.*

All of *Dust Tracks* must be taken with caution. Hurston became an accomplished "liar" who also spun her tales to suit her purposes, became an accomplished artist who also crafted her work to satisfy her imagination. Poised between two worlds—the black South of her childhood and the white North of her education and adulthood—she constructed the statue of herself that she permitted the world to see. The Northern education and, in its wake, membership in the literate culture of the nation shaped her expectations of her readers and, in some measure, shaped her representation of herself. But she never completely weeded out her Southern roots. As she herself maintained, "In the first place, I was a Southerner, and had the map of Dixie on my tongue" (135). And then, she was always "Mama's child" (91), even if she notes that her Mama, alarmed by Zora's tendency to wander, could not understand that some "children are just bound to take after their fathers in spite of women's prayers" (32).

Like Janie in *Their Eyes Were Watching God,* Hurston returns from the horizon transformed to establish herself in the male preserve of tale-telling. As the teller of her tale, she transcends her gender-specific discourse in her interpretive community. To the extent that she speaks in the language of that community, she does as an outsider rather than a member. Her trip to the horizon has given her new eyes and ears. She speaks her native tongue as an interpreter. We might say that only her exposure to another discourse has permitted her to tell her story. Without that exposure, the story would have been a life, not a story at all. The same could be said of *Dust Tracks.* But, recognizing *Dust Tracks* as a story, we must also recognize it as, in some measure, a lie. A frequently glorious, frequently disquieting lie, but a lie nonetheless. And somewhere in *Dust Tracks* lies buried the fear that, as her white god-father told her, prompts people to lie.

"I hadn't so much forgot as I couldn't bring myself to remember" (3). *I Know Why the Caged Bird Sings* begins with memory and its lapses. Maya

Angelou represents her young self as unable to remember the remainder of a poem. The poem that the younger self could not remember began, "What are you looking at me for? I didn't come to stay . . ." (3). The line she could not remember went, "I just come to tell you, it's Easter Day" (5). Angelou thus opens *Caged Bird* under the aegis of memory, truth, and passing through. The "n[o]t stay[ing]" of the poem recited by the children in the Colored Methodist Episcopal Church in Stamps, Arkansas, referred to the reality of resurrection from the brevity and immateriality of life on this troubled earth to a better life. Yet in Angelou's hands, the poem also evokes a secular meaning. Surely, her younger self had not come to Stamps to stay. Was she not merely passing time before rejoining her parents, claiming her birthright, embarking on a better life?

For the young Marguerite, the birthright she would one day claim is her own whiteness. Watching her grandmother make her dress for that Easter day, she had known "that once I put it on I'd look like a movie star," would "look like one of the sweet little white girls who were everybody's dream of what was right with the world." But the light of Easter morning harshly reveals the magic dress to be only "a plain ugly cut-down from a white woman's once-was-purple throwaway." Yet Marguerite clings to the truth of her own resurrection: "Wouldn't they be surprised when one day I woke out of my black ugly dream . . . ?" (4). It was all a dreadful mistake. "Because I was really white and because a cruel fairy stepmother, who was understandably jealous of my beauty, had turned me into a too-big Negro girl, with nappy black hair, broad feet and a space between her teeth that would hold a number two pencil" (4–5). And Angelou, the narrator, notes, bringing her adult knowledge to bear on the memories, "If growing up is painful for the Southern Black girl, being aware of her displacement is the rust on the razor that threatens the throat. It is an unnecessary insult" (6).

In *Caged Bird,* Angelou sifts through the pain to reappropriate—on her own terms—that Southern past and to undo the displacement. Her highly crafted, incandescent text selectively explores the intertwining relations of origins and memory to her identity. The unrecognized whiteness of the child she represents herself as having been gives way to the proud blackness of the woman she has become. The pride is the pride of a survivor, of history repossessed. That "the adult American Negro female emerges a formidable character," she insists, should be "accepted as an inevitable outcome of the struggle won by survivors" (265).

In her brief opening prologue, Angelou establishes both her perspective as adult narrator—the survivor of the memories of which she is writing—and the perspective of the child she recollects herself as having been. As child she presumably experienced the world around her in a seamless flow, punctuated by disconnected fragments, like a young girl's traumatic inability to control her urine. The adult narrator captures the emblematic memories, vivid and compelling in themselves, and weaves them together to illustrate and anchor the truth of the story as a whole. The prologue thus offers a concrete identification of the protagonist as black, Southern female—the interpreter of her own experience, the teller of her own story.

The "I"—Marguerite Johnson, nicknamed My (later expanded to Maya) by her beloved brother Bailey—was not born in the South. When she was three and Bailey four they arrived there wearing tags, "'To Whom It May Concern'" (6). Uprooted by the collapse of their parents' "calamitous" marriage, they had been shipped home to their father's mother, whom they called "Momma" (6–7). Angelou locates that trip in relation to the experience of the other frightened black children who must also have crossed the United States thousands of times, in relation to the social consequences of some blacks' migration northward during the early decades of the twentieth century. The consequences of that migration wrested Maya and Bailey, like countless others, from their mother, who remained in the North to attempt to make a living amidst the debris of the fractured expectations of easy affluence. But it hardly left them "motherless," as the black women who befriended them on the Southern lap of their journey would have had it. For their grandmother closed the gap in the generations by becoming their Momma, and her town, after recognizing them as "harmless (and children)," responded to them by closing "in around us, as a real mother embraces a stranger's child. Warmly, but not too familiarly" (7)

Angelou represents the ten years (interrupted by a brief and fateful period with her mother in St. Louis), from three to thirteen, that she spent under Momma's care in Stamps as the core of her childhood and, implicitly, as the wellspring of her adult identity. Through her evocations of Stamps she links herself to the Southern roots and history of her people—to a succession of American Negro female survivors whom she implicitly credits with laying the foundations for her own survival. But that core includes an inescapable harshness that weaves through Angelou's text, structuring the memories, containing the faith, gentleness, and mutual concern that kept its worst consequences at bay, even as it sorely tried them. Stamps, for all its black core of loving security, bred paranoia. "Stamps, Arkansas, was Chitlin' Switch, Georgia; Hang 'Em High, Alabama; Don't Let the Sun Set on You Here, Nigger, Mississippi; or any other name just as descriptive." The people of Stamps "used to say that whites in our town were so prejudiced that a Negro couldn't buy vanilla ice cream. Except on July Fourth. Other days he had to be satisfied with chocolate" (47). Stamps also bred the deep solidarity of the black community that gathered in Momma's store to listen to the broadcast of Joe Louis's fight with Carnera, listen without breathing, without hoping, just waiting. Life-defying, suspenseful minutes later Louis had won. "Champion of the world. A Black boy. Some Black mother's son." But the triumphant crowd disperses slowly, with caution. "It wouldn't do for a Black man and his family to be caught on a lonely country road on a night when Joe Louis had proved that we were the strongest people in the world" (132).

Nor would it do for a black woman to ask a white dentist, who owes her the money that had saved his practice during the Depression, to treat her suffering granddaughter. "'Annie,'" he met Momma's desperate plea, "'my policy is I'd rather stick my hand in a dog's mouth than in a nigger's'" (184). Nor would it do for black children to aspire to any but a utilitarian education. Marguerite's graduation from eighth grade—a momentous occasion for the community as well as the graduates—dawns with the promise of perfection, but its perfection shatters with the appearance of the visiting white commencement speaker from Texarkana. Promising the white children (of whom there were none in the audience) the most advanced educational opportunities, he praises the black children (the graduating class that he is addressing) for having sent a "first-line football tackler" to Arkansas Agricultural and Mechanical College, a terrific basketball player to Fisk. "The white kids were going to have a chance to become Galileos and Madame Curies and Edisons and Gauguins, and our boys (the girls weren't even in on it) would try to be Jessie Owenses and Joe Louises" (174). Marguerite and her classmates, drawers of meticulous maps, spellers of decasyllabic words, memorizers of the whole of *The Rape of Lucrece,* have been exposed as "maids and farmers, handymen and washerwomen" (175–176). How, amidst such ugliness, could Henry Reed even think of delivering his valedictory address, "To Be Or Not To Be?" Hadn't he understood anything? Henry, "the conservative, the proper, the A student," has understood everything. Completing his prepared address as if dreams still have meaning, he turns his back to the audience, faces his class, and singing, nearly speaking, he intones, "'Lift ev'ry voice and sing / Till earth and heaven ring / Ring with the harmonies of Liberty. . . .'" Henry understands. "It was the poem written by James Weldon Johnson. It was the music composed by J. Rosamond Johnson. It was the Negro national anthem. Out of habit we were singing it" (178). And singing the song that she, like every other black child had learned with her ABCs, Marguerite hears it for the first time. By the close of the singing, they "were on top again. As always, again. We survived. The depths had been icy and dark, but now a bright sun spoke to our souls. I was no longer simply a member of the proud graduating class of 1940; I was a proud member of the wonderful, beautiful Negro race" (179).

Shortly after graduation, Momma decides that Marguerite and Bailey are to join their mother in California. Stamps is no place for an ambitious black boy, no place, although she never says so, for an ambitious black girl. Marguerite's previous trip away from Stamps, her previous stay with her mother, offered no grounds for believing that the world beyond Stamps is safer. During that stay in Saint Louis, Marguerite had been raped by the man with whom her mother was living. Withal, Angelou does not represent that rape, which racked the eight-year-old girl's body with unbearable pain, as the worst. The worst occurred during the subsequent trial of the rapist at which Marguerite, forced to testify, lied. Under examination she felt compelled to say that Mr. Freeman had never tried to touch her before the rape, although he had and she believed she had encouraged him to. That lie "lumped in my throat and I couldn't get air" (82). On the basis of that lie Mr. Freeman was convicted. In fact, the lie did not cause Mr. Freeman to serve time; his lawyer got him released. It did cause his death. No sooner had he been released than her mother's brothers killed him. To Marguerite, "a man was dead because I lied. . . . Obviously I had forfeited my place in heaven forever. . . . I could feel the evilness flowing through my body and waiting, pent up, to rush off my tongue if I tried to open my mouth. I clamped my teeth shut, I'd hold it in" (84).

In the wake of the trial, Marguerite and Bailey were sent back to Stamps, where for nearly a year Marguerite persisted in her silence. Then, Mrs. Bertha Flowers, "the aristocrat of Black Stamps," threw her a life line. Mrs. Flowers "was one of the few gentlewomen I have ever known, and has remained throughout my life the measure of what a human being can be" (91). From the start, Mrs. Flowers appealed to her because she was like "women in English novels who walked the moors (whatever they were) with their loyal dogs racing at a respectful distance." Above all, "she made me proud to be a Negro, just by being herself" (92). Mrs. Flowers joined the world of Stamps to the world of literature, embodied in her person the dreams that shaped Marguerite's imagination. For Marguerite, under Mrs. Flowers's tutelage, formal education became salvation. But even as she introduced Marguerite to the delights of *Tale of Two Cities*, Mrs. Flowers enjoined her to recognize the beauties and sense of black folk culture. Ignorance and illiteracy, she insisted, should not be confused. "She encouraged me to listen carefully to what country people call mother wit. That in those homely sayings was couched the collective wisdom of generations" (97). Language, the human form of communication, alone separates man from the lower animals. Words, she insisted, have a life beyond the printed page. Words, even written words, acquire meaning by being spoken. Books should be read aloud. Angelou thus represents Mrs. Flowers as bridging the gap between oral and literary culture, between the black community of Stamps and Jane Eyre.[8] Under Mrs. Flowers's influence, Marguerite again began to speak.

Southern roads and cages. Hurston and Angelou knew them well, but represented them differently. The differences reflect differences in generation—the Harlem Renaissance, the 1960s—but also something more. Hurston apparently did not find it easy to connect her Southern past to her Northern present, to connect the little black girl to the adult author. To reclaim her past, Hurston, much like a performer or a trickster, had to dish it up as a fable for others' consumption. The Eatonville of her youth became, in her hands, a mythic land immune to time and place, became an Atlantis, a garden of Eden. But by so reconstructing Eatonville, Hurston confessed her own exile. With her mother's death and the beginnings of her wanderings, that earlier world ended. Hurston thus represents herself as cut free from her moorings, which she could only repossess through the foreign tongue of the literati.

Angelou depends no less than Hurston on that foreign tongue. But unlike her, she insists upon the connections. Less afraid than Hurston of the burden of her people's history, she anchors herself in that history. Less afraid than Hurston of her own anger at racism and oppression, she insists upon their persistence. Openly proclaiming the "lifelong paranoia" that Stamps forced upon her, she can also claim her kinship with generations of black female survivors. No less a denizen of the Republic of Letters than Hurston, Angelou claims her rightful place as a woman—a black woman. For Hurston's myth, she substitutes history and thereby claims her specific identity.

It all comes back to the South. But it also comes back to lies. For Hurston, lying represented the magic of men's tales, the delights of crafted deception, even if, on her own telling, lying also masked fear. No less than Hurston, Angelou recognized lying as the mask of fear, but for her lying led not to stories but to imposed silence. To write her story—to speak at all—she had to conquer the fear, repudiate the lie. Hurston's South instructed her in the necessity of lying to preserve the self from violence, denial, and death, but in her glorious "lies" she denied the knowledge, transformed the fearful reality into a death-defying myth. To be heard at all she felt obliged to represent herself in black face—a spoofing, harmless minstrel. The lessons of Angelou's South were no less harsh, but including as they did the faith of Momma, the courage of Henry Reed, and the teachings of Mrs. Flowers, they also taught her that the South need not be wrapped in mythical denial. It could be claimed as the legacy of the people—especially the woman—who had taught her how to survive and to sing.

Notes

1. Excellent examples of white Southern women's devotion to the Southern landscape can be found in Augusta J. Evans's novels *Beulah* (1859) and *Macaria* (1862).

2. Andrews, in *To Tell a Free Story*, emphasizes nineteenth-century African-Americans' concern with freedom in their self-representations, but the relation between freedom and the independent self figures in most discussions of the slave narrative. See, for example, Sekora and Turner; Davis and Gates; Foster; Smith, *Where I'm Bound*; Baker; and Stepto. The theme of freedom and selfhood was unquestionably important to Frederick Douglass and Harriet Jacobs. See Martin;

Yellin's introduction to *Jacobs's Incidents;* and my epilogue to *Within the Plantation Household.*

3. Barbara McCaskill offers a pioneering exploration of the relations between African-American women's self-representations and the expectations of their readerships. Henry Louis Gates's welcome 30-volume *Schomburg Library* offers a newly coherent picture of African-American women's writings, and the authors of the introductions to the discrete volumes offer important discussions of the specific texts.

4. I have offered a fuller discussion of the nature of African-American women's experience and self-representations in relation to gender, especially their sense of gender identity, in "To Write My Self" and *Within the Plantation Household.*

5. For a thorough and thoughtful discussion of black folk culture, see Levine. For examples of white evocation of black dialect, see Harriet Beecher Stowe's *Uncle Tom's Cabin* (1852). Significantly, Jacobs, in *Incidents,* represents slave women on the plantation as speaking in dialect, but herself as speaking perfect "white" English.

6. Throughout, I am distinguishing between Hurston, the narrator or autobiographer, and Zora, her former self; between Angelou, narrator or autobiographer, and Marguerite, her former self. For one of the many discussions of the problem of the autobiographical narrator, see Smith's *A Poetics of Women's Autobiography.* For my own views on the general problem of autobiography and additional references, see my edition of *The Autobiography of Du Pont de Nemours.*

7. On Hurston's notorious inaccuracy, see Hemenway's introduction to the second edition of *Dust Tracks;* on some of the problems of that inaccuracy, see my essay "My Statue, My Self," on Hurston's ambiguous forms of address, see Johnson; and on Hurston's life, see Hemenway's *Zora Neale Hurston.*

8. *Jane Eyre* was Marguerite's favorite novel, as *Huckleberry Finn* was Bailey's, and Angelou mentions it frequently in *Caged Bird.*

Works Cited

Andrews, William L. *To Tell a Free Story: The First Century of Afro-American Autobiography,* 1760–1865. Urbana: University of Illinois Press, 1986.

Angelou, Maya. *I Know Why the Caged Bird Sings.* New York: Random House, 1969.

Baker, Houston A., Jr. *The Journey Back: Issues in Black Literature and Criticism.* Chicago: University of Chicago Press, 1980.

Davis, Charles, and Henry Louis Gates, Jr., eds. *The Slave's Narrative.* New York: Oxford University Press, 1985.

Foster, Frances Smith. *Witnessing Slavery: The Development of Ante-Bellum Slave Narratives.* Westport: Greenwood, 1919.

Fox-Genovese, Elizabeth, ed. & trans. *The Autobiography of Du Pont de Nemours.* Wilmington: Scholarly, 1984.

———. "My Statue, My Self: Autobiographical Writings of Afro-American Women." *The Private Self: Theory and Practice of Women's Autobiographical Writings.* Ed. Shari Benstock. Chapel Hill: University of North Carolina Press, 1988. 63–89.

———. "To Write My Self: The Autobiographical Writings of Afro-American Women." *Feminist Issues in Literary Scholarship.* Ed. Shari Benstock. Bloomington: Indiana University Press, 1987. 161–180.

———. *Within the Plantation Household: Black and White Women of the Old South.* Chapel Hill: University of North Carolina Press, 1988.

Gates, Henry Louis, Jr., ed. *The Schomburg Library of Nineteenth-Century Black Women Writers*. 30 vols. New York: Oxford University Press, 1988.

Hemenway, Robert E. *Zora Neale Hurston: A Literary Biography*. Urbana: University of Illinois Press, 1978.

Hurston, Zora Neale. *Dust Tracks on a Road: An Autobiography*. Ed. Robert E. Hemenway. 2nd ed. Urbana: University of Illinois Press, 1984.

Jacobs, Harriet. *Incidents in the Life of a Slave Girl*. Ed. Jean Fagin Yellin. Cambridge: Harvard University Press, 1987.

Johnson, Barbara. *A World of Difference*. Baltimore: Johns Hopkins University Press, 1987.

Levine, Lawrence. *Black Culture and Black Consciousness: Afro-American Folk Thought from Slavery to Freedom*. New York: Oxford University Press, 1977.

Martin, Waldo E., Jr. *The Mind of Frederick Douglass*. Chapel Hill: University of North Carolina Press, 1984.

McCaskill, Barbara. "An Eternity for Telling: Topological Traditions in Afro-American Women's Writing." Dissertation, Emory University, 1988.

Sekora, John, and Darwin T. Turner, eds. *The Art of Slave Narrative: Original Essays in Criticism and Theory*. Macomb: Western Illinois University, 1982.

Smith, Sidonie. *A Poetics of Women's Autobiography: Marginality and the Fictions of Self-Representation*. Bloomington: Indiana University Press, 1987.

———. *Where I'm Bound: Patterns of Slavery and Freedom in Black American Autobiography*. Westport: Greenwood, 1974.

Stepto, Robert B. *From Behind the Veil: A Study of Afro-American Narrative*. Urbana: University of Illinois Press, 1979.

BONNIE BRAENDLIN

A (Sub)version of the American Dream in Maya Angelou's
I Know Why the Caged Bird Sings

In a 1973 interview with Bill Moyers, Maya Angelou had the following exchange:

MOYERS: . . . You've really been a mobile, nomadic, free person. What price have you paid for that freedom?

ANGELOU: Well, at some point—you only are free when you realize you belong no place—you belong every place—no place at all. The price is high. The reward is great.

MOYERS: Do you belong anywhere?

ANGELOU: I haven't yet.

MOYERS: Do you belong to anyone?

ANGELOU: More and more. I mean, I belong to myself.

This interview suggests a major theme of *I Know Why the Caged Bird Sings*, the first volume of Angelou's autobiography, namely that of learning how to belong to herself and not to others. The theme emerges from a process of self-development that allows the African-American woman to be free only if she refuses to capitulate to a destiny determined by societal racism and

Middle Atlantic Writers' Association (MAWA) Review, Volume 6, Number 1 (June 1991): pp. 4–6. © 1991 Bonnie Braendlin.

sexism. Published in 1970, on the cusp between the civil rights and women's liberation movements, this book is one of many texts that signal African-American women's resistance to being forced into positions of silence in the margins of discourse and of powerlessness on the bottom rungs of the American social hierarchy. Abena Busia expresses their goal during and after this liberation era:

> [W]hat we are undertaking is a process of affirmation, to proclaim that selfhood, our very own, which has heretofore been "othered."
> . . . As black women we have recognized the need to rewrite or to reclaim our own *her*stories, and to define ourselves. (1)

Angelou speaks for liberated women of her time, but in order to show the pervasiveness and persistence of oppression in America, she displaces the struggle for voice, place and selfhood back to the era of her childhood, the 1940s and 50s, when racism and sexism were powerful, overt deterrents to selfhood and social progress. Children in that era learned very early where they belonged in a supremacist society and for the most part they accepted rather than protest or refuse their places. In *Caged Bird* Maya expresses her own particular plight as that of the triple oppression experienced by all black women:

> The Black female is assaulted in her tender years by all those common forces of nature at the same time that she is caught in the tripartite crossfire of masculine prejudice, white illogical hate and Black lack of power. (231)

Moving her younger self from an opening position of displaced orphan in the deep South to a place of responsibility as the first black streetcar conductor in San Francisco, Angelou follows the Horatio Alger pattern of rags to riches which infuses the American Dream. Her appropriation of a white male plan for success "signifies" (to borrow Henry Louis Gates' term) upon a dominate culture tactic which proffers the Dream to everyone while simultaneously denying it to some, thus excluding them from the Dream's rewards. By shifting the rights and privileges inherent in the Horatio Alger text from the white male to the black female, Angelou achieves a power play that helps to rewrite individual and group destiny in the American liberation era.

African-American women, like all women, must of necessity live in a supremacist society; thus their determination to belong to the mainstream while defining positions of resistance is fraught with danger. Hence, as Angelou suggests in *Caged Bird*, they must develop strategies that insure survival and success, while permitting subversion. Angelou's autobiographical voice is personal yet representative of the black American woman as it both speaks and resists an identity imposed by society to which she both does and does not belong; in *Caged Bird* she creates a black female self who is positioned in society but is constantly in flux. When Maya eventually achieves a place of earning power in a society bent on silencing and even murdering her, she does so by adopting strategies learned from the black subculture, represented by her mother, father, stepfather, and their con men acquaintances, strategies of lying, signifyin', and traveling on, which through subversion claim for Maya the privileges of truth and place which her society denies her.

Angelou's tactics, the reasons for their use, and the results become clearer if we view this first volume of her autobiography as a combination of *Bildungsroman* and picaresque fiction, the one suggesting integration by compromise and consent, the other signaling resistance by dissent. Until the American liberation era, the *Bildungsroman* was pretty much a white male (and occasionally white female) genre. During the 1960s and 70s, however, men and women of color wrote self-development novels to position themselves within the mainstream while expressing ethnic pride and recovering lost origins.

The first two-thirds of *Caged Bird*, depicting the growth and development of Marguerite Johnson (later Maya Angelou) in Stamps, Arkansas, from age three to seventeen, may be read as a *Bildungsroman* or coming-of-age story. Defined as a novel of formation of personality or identity, the *Bildungsroman* explores an individual's shaping of him- or herself, and being shaped, by making choices (or sometimes non-choices) among various roles determined by social and cultural ideologies, expressed by various discourses, for example, education, religion, the law and the media. As an "education-into-life" novel, the *Bildungsroman* reflects or represents the socialization process during which the child grows up learning what her culture expects her to be; proper roles and positions within discourses are taught to the developing child by parents, mentors, and socially approved texts and media. Adolescents may resist prescribed roles and identities in the name of personal freedom and idealistic desires, but finally are persuaded through the efforts of mentors and friends to conform, thus earning the reward of a "rightful" place in society, often designated by "proper" vocational and marital choices. Traditional *Bildungsromane* like *David Copperfield* and *Jane Eyre* see their protagonists happily situated in business and marriage, privileged positions in bourgeois capitalism.

As a child Maya voraciously reads many of the major authors in the British-American canon, her favorites being Shakespeare and Edgar Allan Poe. But one of the texts that she rereads, especially in times of stress, is *Jane Eyre*. No doubt Maya identifies with Jane Eyre as a misunderstood and abused child, whose unjust punishments are eventually requited, and thus she finds both solace and escapism in rereading Jane's story. *Jane Eyre* follows the trajectory of a fairy tale, beginning with a poor child, often a girl and an orphan, who suffers ostracism and brutality in situations that polarize good and evil; she is ultimately rescued by a fairy godmother or a prince, whereupon she is disclosed to be a real princess after all. She and the prince, of course, live happily ever after. The displacement of fairy tales to the novel sees Jane as vulnerable because she has no money and no social position, as persecuted by a stepmother and a cruel schoolmaster but aided by a kind teacher, cast into the moors by the wicked rogue Rochester and finally rescued by her "real" family and elevated to her proper place in life by an inherited fortune, from whence she is able to marry her "true love," now contrite and reformed.

At the beginning of *Caged Bird* Maya is also a kind of orphan, abandoned by her parents; but, unlike Jane, Maya is loved and cared for by her grandmother, Momma Henderson, and she is educated by Mrs. Flowers, a mentor figure who restores Maya's sense of herself as a person and her power of language after the cruel and brutalizing rape and trial in St. Louis. Like Jane, Maya is cast out of her milieu in a crisis situation; when her brother Bailey is traumatized by the drowned black man, Maya and Bailey are taken by Momma out of the deep South to the relative freedom of California, an incident to which I shall make future reference. But Maya never expects to be rescued by a prince and she doesn't wind up happily married to a protective father figure, as Jane does; instead Maya becomes an unwed mother, whose bonding with her child at the end of *Caged Bird* helps to undermine the privileged sanctity of bourgeois marriage and motherhood which characterizes traditional female *Bildungsromane*.

In addition to reading female success stories like *Jane Eyre*, Maya is influenced by Horatio Alger tales:

> I spent most of my Saturdays at the library [no interruptions] breathing in the world of penniless shoeshine boys who, with goodness and perseverance, became rich, rich men, and gave baskets of goodies to the poor on holidays. (*CB* 641)

Isolated in a racially segregated small town, young Maya has some idea of the realities of the American social hierarchy with its rigid demarcations between the haves and the have nots, but segregation also feeds her desire for material goods denied her by the blacks' abject poverty:

> A light shade had been pulled down between the Black community and all things white, but one could see through it enough to develop a fear-admiration contempt for the white "things" . . . [A]bove all, their wealth . . . was the most enviable. (*CB* 40)

Interestingly enough, it is Momma who serves as a model of economic success for Maya to emulate: Momma owns a store, which survives the depression, even though "her customers had no money" (41); she loans money to whites and proves to be baffling to the judge who calls her *Mrs.* Henderson because she is a store owner, even though as a black, she has no right in his eyes to the title.

Up until her middle school graduation, Maya believes that her education will give her the cultural literacy necessary to succeed in the material world. But her dreams of climbing the success ladder are cruelly shattered when the commencement speaker, a white man from the big world beyond Stamps and a representative of American supremacy, informs the children of their predetermined destinies:

> The White kids were going to have a chance to become Galileos and Madame Curies and Edisons and Gauguins, and our boys (the girls weren't even in on it) would try to be Jesse Owenses and Joe Louises. . . . We were maids and farmers, handymen and washerwomen, and anything higher that we aspired to was farcical and presumptuous. (151–152)

Maya's realization of the disparity between her desire to participate in the American Dream and denial of that desire by society that defines her as inferior ruptures her euphoric pride in her education and plunges her into despair: "It was awful to be Negro and have no control over my life" (153).

The incident which shatters the *Bildungsroman* trajectory of *Caged Bird* and explodes the text into the picaresque chaos is the discovery of the drowned black man, which traumatizes Bailey and forces Momma into the realization that her beloved grandchildren are not physically safe in the overtly racist South, especially because neither Bailey nor Maya seems likely to adopt the survivalist stance of her generation, that of silent submissiveness. So she displaces the children yet again, this time to California to live with their mother and stepfather Daddy Clidell and, alternately, with their birth father. In the beginning of *Caged Bird* Maya voices the *Southern Black girl's* acute awareness of "her displacement [as] the rust on the razor that threatens the throat" (3), but in the last third of the book, as she becomes a picara in California, she revels in the "air of collective displacement, the impermanence of life in wartime" that allows her a freedom and anonymity in a relatively unsegregated community denied to her in Stamps. As a picara, Maya learns strategies which turn the tables on racist ultimatums, allowing her access to the forbidden American Dream and on her own terms.

Works Cited

Angelou, Maya. "A Conversation with Maya Angelou." With Bill Moyers. *Conversation with Maya Angelou*. Ed. Jeffrey M. Elliot. Jackson and London: University Press of Mississippi, 1989.

———. *I Know Why the Caged Bird Sings*. 1970. New York: Bantam, 1985.

Busia, Abena P. B. "Words Whispered over Voids: A Context for Black Women's Rebellious Voices in the Novel of the African Diaspora." *Black Feminist Criticism and Critical Theory*. Ed. Joe Weixlmann and Houston A. Baker, Jr. *Studies in Black American Literature*, Vol. III. Greenwood, Florida: Penkevill, 1988. 1–41.

IAN MARSHALL

Why the Caged Bird Laughs: Humor in Maya Angelou's I Know Why the Caged Bird Sings

As her title suggests, Maya Angelou in the autobiography of her childhood *I Know Why the Caged Bird Sings* demonstrates that one can find and express freedom and joy even amid social constraints—in her case the constraints created by the oppression of racism and the insecurity of childhood and adolescence. In truth, though, the book's most frequent act and symbol of joyful liberation is not song but laughter. On a rough count, I found 35 references to music or song, compared to 91 mentions of laughter; 17 smiles; nine giggles, nine mentions of jokes or joking; seven references to something being funny; two instances each of something being amusing, humorous, or mocking; two grins; one mention each of gaiety, jollity and comedy; and a smirk, a titter, a snicker, and a cackle. The book echoes with laughter, its course and function varying from page to page. It is a veritable treatise on the varieties of the comedic experience. At times laughter is a means of oppression—in the form of taunting, teasing, and mocking. In this sense, it serves as a means of exclusion, and it is employed by adults in their dealings with children as well as by southern whites in their dealings with Blacks. Used in the same manner, but in other hands, laughter is a means of claiming revenge, or of asserting pride. It can be a means of approval and inclusion, as a way of defining an in-group that may be segregated from society's mainstream. In short, laughter and humor are used offensively and

Middle Atlantic Writers' Association (MAWA) Review, Volume 6, Number 1 (June 1991): pp. 7–10. © 1991 Ian Marshall.

49

defensively, as a means of attacking and as a means of coping; or, as Sandy Cohen puts it in speaking of racial and ethnic humor in general, humor can be either a "weapon" or a "tool" (203). And it is presented from the point of view of both victim and victor, butt of the joke and jokester. Thus the laughter in the book delineates both the affliction of oppression and the coping strategies by which Angelou gains self-esteem amid the tribulations of female adolescence and the humiliations of racism.

The book's preface signals the importance of laughter in the book to come and suggests the shift in its significance that will accompany Angelou's maturation. The book opens with Marguerite, as she is called as a child, finding herself unable to complete a recitation in church, conscious that the other children are "wiggling and giggling" over her "well-known forgetfulness" (1). Of course, the children's laughter is undoubtedly the cause as well as the result of her forgetfulness. At this stage, and through much of the early part of the book, laughter serves as a means of torment. But at the end of the preface, a scant two pages after her initial humiliation, Angelou describes herself running from the church, peeing herself and crying, aware that the other kids will have "something new to tease [her] about" and that she'll "get a whipping" from her grandmother for running out of church—and despite all this she herself is laughing, "partially for the sweet release," she says, but still more for "being liberated from the silly church [and] from the knowledge that [she] shouldn't die from a busted head" (3). As in this incident, through the course of the book laughter becomes more a means of coping with humiliation, of freeing herself from constraints (be they physical or perceptual), and of delighting in her capacity to survive and even thrive amid torment and humiliation.

Most often the humiliation comes at the hands of whites, and often laughter is their weapon. When some white girls visit Maya's grandmother's store in Stamps, Arkansas, their laughter is evoked by their mimickry of Maya's grandmother, the guardian whom Maya knows as "Momma." The girls challenge Momma's authority as adult by impudently exposing their privates while doing handstands in front of the store. Maya's instinct is to go for a rifle, or "to throw a handful of black pepper in their faces, to throw lye on them, to scream that they were dirty, scummy peckerwoods" (25)—in other words, to return pain with pain. At this point she has not yet learned to employ humor either as a means of revenge or as a coping strategy; she is conscious only that humor is a means of inflicting painful humiliation. Momma's reaction to the incident is to withstand the abuse, stolidly and implacably heroic in her refusal to be riled or ridiculed. She remains victoriously placid, even beatific; Maya describes Momma's face as "a brown moon that shone on me" (26).

Though Maya discerns the victory of sorts in Momma's reaction, she has not yet learned Momma's techniques of enduring abuse. Nor has she learned to avoid ridiculing others as she would have them avoid ridiculing her. In the very next chapter, she employs humor as a means of ridicule in much the same way that her tormentors had. When the ugly, fat, and presumptuous Reverend Thomas comes to visit, looking for his usual free meal, Maya and her brother Bailey delight in their imitations of him, much as the white girls had giggled over their mimickry of Momma. Most of the chapter, one of the funniest in the book, focuses on an incident in church, when Sister Monroe interrupts the Reverend's sermon with enthusiastic cries to "Preach it!" She chases him out of the pulpit and through the church, continually calling for him to "Preach it!", finally catches him and, while he is in mid-expostulation, whacks him in the back of the head with her purse. His false teeth, still grinning, pop out of his head, "looking empty," writes, Angelou, "and at the same time to contain all the emptiness of the world" (36). Despite the poignancy of the description, and despite her fear of furthering the disruption in church, Maya laughs uncontrollably. She justifies her laughter by remarking on the Reverend's lack of embarrassment and his sustained pomposity as he continues his sermon sans teeth. But still, her laughter is aimed at a victim, and she uses it as a weapon. Perhaps the adult Angelou is conscious of the threat posed by such a use of humor, for she closes the chapter by commenting that her laughter was close to hysteria, and for weeks afterward she "stood on laughter's cliff," where "any funny thing could hurl [her] off to her death far below" (37). The image of danger suggests that laughter threatens not just the butt of the joke, but the victimizing jokester herself.

In the Sister Monroe incident, Maya and her brother's laughter is unwarranted, cruel even, for Reverend Thomas is targeted merely for being pompous and taking the best meat at Maya's dinner table; Sister Monroe is guilty of religious enthusiasm. As Maya begins to mature, her humor becomes more purposeful and justifiable, especially as it serves to exact revenge. When she works as a maid for a Mrs. Cullinan, she is humiliated by her employer's inability and then refusal to get her name right. Mrs. Cullinan at first calls her "Margaret" instead of "Marguerite," an insult which is compounded when a friend of hers, whom Maya refers to as a "speckled-faced" woman, advises Mrs. Cullinan that "Margaret" is too long and that she should call Maya "Mary." Apparently, this sort of renaming is standard practice in the South, for Mrs. Cullinan's other maid confides to Maya that her original given name was "Hallelujah," but she was renamed "Glory" by her mistress. A sign of Maya's increasing sensitivity is that she restrains the impulse either to laugh at the absurd names or to cry at Miss Glory's appalling acquiescence in the loss of her identity. To get herself fired, Maya drops Mrs. Cullinan's favorite china—accidentally on purpose, right in front of her employer. When the speckled-faced woman comes in to see the broken plates and Mrs. Cullinan crying over them, she asks, "Who did it, Viola? Was it Mary? Who did it?" In an outburst that reveals the effectiveness of Maya's vengeful ploy, Mrs. Cullinan bursts out, "Her name's Margaret, goddamn it, her name's Margaret!" She throws a shard of the broken china at Maya, but hits poor Miss Glory instead. When Maya tells the story to her brother, they "burst out laughing" when she gets to the part where Mrs. Cullinan "screwed up her ugly face to cry" (92).

Maya's laughter in this incident may be cruel, at least insofar as Mrs. Cullinan is the target, but the laughter seems warranted as a viable response to oppression when few other means of rebellion are available. As a black adolescent girl working for a white mistress in the deep South of the 1930s, what can Maya do to subvert the system except drop plates and laugh? As Richard Barksdale notes in "Black America and the Mask of Comedy," humor provides psychological compensation for oppression when no real shift in power is possible (351).

Later in *Caged Bird,* that sort of psychological compensation becomes less of a personal matter and more of a social concern. That is, Maya's laughter is evoked by tales of revenge not for personal affronts but for affronts to her race, a sign that her sensitivity extends beyond the self. While living with her mother in San Francisco, Maya meets her stepfather's circle of friends, a group of con artists with names like Just Black, Cool Clyde, Red Leg, and Stonewall Jimmy. Maya delights in their stories because in their con games "the Black man . . . won out every time over the powerful, arrogant white" (187). It is, in fact, the very power and arrogance of their white targets that make these con men so successful, for they play on white hatred of Blacks and white perceptions of Black stupidity. The example Angelou gives is of a white con artist who specialized in bilking African-Americans, but who himself becomes the mark for a con game run by Just Black and Red Leg. Just Black approaches the mark, saying that he has heard that the mark is one white man who can be trusted. Since his reputation does not at all warrant such trust, the mark has to be incredibly arrogant to believe that his con games have succeeded so well that none of his victims are aware that they have been conned, and he must believe that his black victims are incredibly stupid not to have caught on. But that is precisely what he believes, and so he also believes Just Black's profession of faith in the mark's reliability. The mark thinks he dupes Just Black and Red Leg by buying valuable land from them for a mere $40,000—but in truth the land is owned by the state. The sense of revenge that Maya feels from hearing stories like this no longer serves to overcome personal humiliation, but to assert racial pride. Though humor is still used as an offensive weapon, the battles being waged with it served a cause larger than personal enmity or spite. Thus the humor of revenge also becomes a means of forming communal bonds. As Konrad Lorenz says of the aggressive nature of humor, "laughter produces simultaneously a strong fellow-feeling among participants and joint aggressiveness against outsiders. . . . Laughter forms a bond and simultaneously draws a line" (253).

Even as the offensive role of laughter changes during the book, from Maya being victim, then victimizer, then avenger, and finally observer of the humor of revenue, laughter takes on a progressively more important value as a mechanism for affirming pride of self, family, and race. It becomes less a means of hurting others or of earning revenge, and more a means of expressing joy or of coping with suffering rather than compensating for it. It becomes laughing *with* rather than laughing *at* someone. When Maya makes her first friend, a girl named Louise, the two girls hold hands and spin around while staring at the sky. Angelou's comment is, "This was surely the time to laugh," and their giggling and "laughing out loud uproariously" is the delightfully silly stuff of unmitigated, unmotivated joy (119)—the joy that bonds friendships. Later, humor becomes a means of strengthening bonds with her mother and step-father. Their sense of humor is one quality that attracts Maya to both of them, and shared laughter provides the means for bringing them all close to another; after living with her mother for only a short while, she says, "What child can resist a mother who laughs freely and often, especially if the child's wit is mature enough to catch the sense of the joke?" (174). Humor then can serve to affirm connections among family, and in this case to mark a step in Maya's progress to maturity. Later, laughter signals her adoption by a new family of sorts, a community of runaways in a southern California junkyard. After spending a night in an abandoned car, she awakes to a "collage of Negro, Mexican and white faces . . . laughing" (214). In these scenes, laughter serves as a sign of acceptance by a carefully delimited in-group of friends, community, or family.

In the funniest scene of the book, the peckerwood dentist scene, humor again *seems* to become an offensive weapon. But Angelou pointedly emphasizes the poignancy of the scene and avoids the easy vengeance of ridicule. When she has a toothache, a local white dentist refuses to treat her because of her color; as he phrases it, "I'd rather stick my hand in a dog's mouth than in a nigger's" (160)—despite the fact that he owes Momma a favor since she had once lent him money. The upshot is that Momma insists on at least getting her loan repaid, with interest, but she and Maya have to drive to Texarkana to see a Black dentist. Maya constructs a fantasy version of what must have happened in Momma's confrontation with the dentist. In language borrowed from romance adventures and western films, Momma—in Maya's fantasy— calls the dentist a "contemptible scoundrel," and she orders him, "now and herewith," to "[l]eave Stamps by sundown." When the dentist humbly thanks her for not killing him, Momma replies, "You're welcome for nothing, you varlet. I wouldn't waste a killing on the likes of you" (162). There is obviously aggression here, but it is played out only in Maya's head. Further, though the passage is full of the humor of incongruity that modern theorists identify as the source of the humorous—incongruity, that is, between the reality of the scene and Maya's conception of it, between Momma's colloquial language and the elevated, bookish rhetoric Maya attributes to her—despite this very apparent humor, Maya does not laugh about it. Afterward, while Momma and Uncle Willie laugh about the retribution Momma exacted from the dentist by demanding interest on her loan, Maya can only comment, sadly, wryly, "I preferred, much preferred my version" (164). Humor here allows Maya to cope with the degradation of racism, but there is no vengeance exacted and no overt savoring of the ridicule of others, even of a callous, hypocritical bigot.

By the end of the book, Maya becomes so expert in employing humor as affirmation rather than aggression that she is no longer affected by potentially humiliating instances where laughter seems to be directed at her. When Maya is worried about her developing sexuality, thinking she might be a lesbian because she has big feet and small breasts, her mother laughs at her concerns. But rather than take the laughter as a taunt or humiliation, Maya is able to share in the laughter at her own expense:

> I knew immediately that she wasn't laughing at me. Or rather than she was laughing at me, but it was something about me that pleased her. The laugh choked a little . . . but finally broke through cleanly. I had to give a small laugh too, although I wasn't tickled at all. But it's mean to watch someone enjoy something and not show your understanding of their enjoyment. (236)

As much as anything in the book, this change in attitude about humor, this shift from perceiving humor as a means of torment seeing it as a means of expressing ties to others and of seeing oneself in perspective, is what marks Maya's progress in her journey from insecurity to mature self-confidence and acceptance of her self, from oppression to joy and liberation.

In the later installments of Angelou's ongoing autobiography, humor remains a prominent (and occasionally *dominant*) motif. In *Gather Together in My Name* (1974), wherein Angelou runs a whorehouse, is rejected by the army and various (mostly married) men, becomes a prostitute for a pimp boyfriend, has her son kidnapped, and is tempted to try hard drugs, the laughter is nervous and defensive and often marijuana-induced; she refers to her attitude as "grinning tolerance" (96). In *Singin' and Swingin' and Gettin' Merry Like Christmas* (1976), the progression in the role of humor is similar to that in *Caged Bird*, though there is little sense of its being used initially as a means of torment. Angelou begins cynical and suspicious, especially of whites, and her laughter, she says, is "a traditional ruse . . . used to shield the Black vulnerability; we laughed to keep from crying" (11). But as she succeeds as a singer and dancer, joining the cast of *Porgy and Bess* on a triumphant European tour, she gains confidence in herself and her people, she becomes less distrustful of others, and more and more the humor becomes joyful and affirming. In *The Heart of a Woman* (1982), Angelou is an accomplished and experienced woman. She runs the New York office for Martin Luther King's Southern Christian Leadership Conference, stars in off-Broadway productions of *Cabaret for Freedom* and Genet's *The Blacks,* marries an African civil rights leader, and works as a journalist in Egypt. She sees through the shallow egalitarianism of liberal whites, she struggles as a writer, her marriage falls apart, and her son is injured in a serious car accident. The tone returns to cynicism, especially regarding race and gender relations, and the laughter becomes subversive. The keynote for Angelou's humor here is taken from a line from Sterling Brown's poem "Strong Men": "We followed away, and laughed as usual. / They heard the laugh and wondered" (43).

The subversive humor evident in *Heart of a Woman* is akin to the humor of revenge that Angelou wields in *Caged Bird* before she finds (temporary) peace with herself. But that peace returns again with the aid of humor, in *All God's Children Need Traveling Shoes* (1986), about Angelou's experience living in Ghana. Humor in this most recent installment of Angelou's ongoing autobiography helps resolve the conflict between Angelou's African-*American* identity and her African heritage. Humor, the message seems to be, provides common ground as a basis for understanding between peoples. As a coping strategy and a means of compensating for suffering, humor has permeated Black American culture; so too is it esteemed in Africa. The president of Liberia proclaims to a friend of Angelou's that in his country "laughter is better than rice" (178). As the book ends, with Angelou leaving Africa to return to America, she realizes that "my people had never completely left Africa. . . . [I]t was Africa which rode in the bulges of our high calves, shook in our protruding behinds and crackled in our wide open laughter" (208). Again, as in *Caged Bird,* laughter becomes a source of liberation, joy, unity, acceptance, connection. The pattern established in the preface to the first volume of Angelou's autobiography is repeated, in ever-widening circles of affirmation, not just in that first book but in the multivolume memoir as a whole.

In an interview, Angelou once summarized the lessons of *I Know Why the Caged Bird Sings,* lessons that seem to be repeated in the books that follow:

> One of the first things that a young person must internalize, deep down in the blood and bones, is the understanding that he may encounter many defeats, but he must not be defeated. If life teaches us anything, it may be that it's even necessary to suffer some defeats. When we look at a diamond, a diamond is the result of extreme pressure. Less pressure, it is crystal; less than that, it is

coal; and less than that, it is fossilized leaves or just plain dirt. It is necessary, therefore, to be tough enough to bite the bullet as it is in fact shot into one's mouth, to bite it and stop it before it tears a hole in one's throat. At the same time, one must learn to care for oneself first, so that one can then dare to care for someone else. That's what it takes to make the caged bird sing. (Elliott 694)

In Angelou's autobiographies, humor seems a necessary precondition for the singing of which she speaks. Humor is a source of character-building pressure as a means of withstanding that pressure; it is a means and a sign of caring for oneself, of coming to terms with oneself, of valuing one's identity; and it is a way of establishing one's connection to others. Like the caged bird singing, the oppressed woman of color affirms the dignity and beauty and joy of life with the melodious sounds of her laughter.

WORKS CITED

Angelou, Maya. *All God's Children Need Traveling Shoes.* New York: Random House, 1986.

———. *Gather Together in My Name.* 1974. New York: Bantam, 1975.

———. *The Heart of a Woman.* 1981. New York: Bantam, 1982.

———. *I Know Why the Caged Bird Sings.* New York: Bantam, 1969.

———. *Singin' and Swingin' and Gettin' Merry Like Christmas.* New York: Random House, 1976.

Barksdale, Richard K. "Black America and the Mask of Comedy." *The Comic Imagination in American Literature.* Ed. Louis D. Rubin. New Brunswick, N.J.: Rutgers University Press, 1973. 349–360.

Cohen, Sandy. "Racial and Ethnic Humor in the United States." *Amerika-Studien/American Studies* 40 (1985): 203–211.

Elliot, Jeffrey M. "Maya Angelou: A Search of Self." *Negro History Bulletin* 40 (1977): 694–695.

Lorenz, Konrad. *On Aggression.* Trans. Marjorie Kerr Wilson. New York: Harcourt, Brace and World, 1963.

MARCIA ANN GILLESPIE

Maya Angelou: Lessons in Living

Some folks you meet leave no impression; Maya Angelou fills up the room. She doesn't speak loudly, doesn't seek to overpower or play the diva to draw attention. She simply is herself. She looks exactly the way I've always imagined many an African queen would: tall, stately, head high, carriage erect, eyes wide, a quiet sense of confidence exuding from her pores. A woman large of frame, she is as at ease with and in her body as she is with the accolades and acclaim that pour in from around the world.

Maya Angelou, the writer, stirred the hearts of millions of readers with her first book, *I Know Why the Caged Bird Sings,* which chronicle her childhood years. In that memoir she shared the trauma of being raped, of her horror at the violence done to her as well as to her assailant, and of becoming mute for several years as a result. But in this, as in all the subsequent memoirs covering her adult years and in her poetry and essays, Maya Angelou has always sought to illume the human experience, to celebrate the human spirit while avoiding mawkish sentimentality—even as she unflinchingly describes her life and ours with clear-eyed detail.

A woman of many parts is Maya Angelou: actress, dancer and director of works for the stage and screen, singer and professor. Her accomplishments are many. For example, she has authored ten books and received 30 honorary doctorates and been nominated for an Emmy Award for her performance in

Essence, Volume 23, Number 8 (December 1992): 48–52. © 1992 Marcia Ann Gillespie.

Roots. She holds a lifetime appointment as a Reynolds Professor of American Studies at Wake Forest University in North Carolina and wrote and hosted the PBS television series *Maya Angelou's America: A Journey of the Heart.* She is one man's mother, one young man's grandmother and mother of the heart to three women. She has been married several times, to men from three continents. She has lived in Cairo, Accra and London and New York, San Francisco and Los Angeles but currently calls Winston Salem, North Carolina, her home.

She is a voracious reader, with nearly photographic recall, and a brilliant raconteur who rarely forgets what she hears. She is a great cook who loves to bring people together around her table. She is a wise woman, her wisdom bred in the bone, honed by experience, built on common sense. Fluent in several languages, she is an intellectual and a scholar, but one who holds sway as easily in a rough-and-tumble bar as in a church, or a college classroom. She is a woman who listens as thoughtfully as she speaks.

I was a young editor, with the big mission of making *Essence* magazine a success, when Maya Angelou first reached out her hand in friendship. I remember she told me how proud she was of me, of what I was doing. I remember too how in awe I was of her, how difficult it was for me to believe that this famous, awesomely talented woman really wanted to be my friend. So I held back, until finally, several years later, Maya invited me to lunch and, in that honest way she has of getting to the heart of the matter, told me that if I wished to be her friend I'd better straighten up and act like a woman, not a little girl. Perhaps it sounds harsh, but it wasn't. We both cried some in that Cuban restaurant that day, and I will always be grateful that she cared enough to reach out again.

I treasure the times I've spent with Maya Angelou. Laughter, yes, there's always plenty of that, and ofttimes tears as well, the kind that come from fullness of spirit and reflect a gamut of emotions. Stories are shared, ideas exchanged in conversations that often range from the bone-personal to the metaphysical to the political. With Maya I am always learning. She teaches by example: how to be more graceful, gracious and giving; how to lovingly call someone to account when necessary and correct without blame or hurt feelings; the importance of giving praise, honor and respect, and of living wholly, fully in the world.

Although I have shared friendship and laughter with this great woman, anyone who reads her memoirs and her poetry, who hears her speak in an auditorium or on a television show, knows who she is as well. What you see or hear or read is no different from what you get from the woman in person, her public face no different than her private one.

This summer I interviewed Maya Angelou in her home. *Essence* editor-in-chief Susan Taylor and her daughter Nequai came down as well. Nequai served as our technical assistant, checking on tapes and adjusting mikes, while my sister-friend Susan made sure we all stayed on track. In Maya Angelou's warm, rambling house, we four women spent many hours together gathered round her table in the big flowing kitchen dining area, savoring Maya's wonderful cooking, sharing life stories, life lessons, life struggles. Afterward, Maya Angelou and I settled into an easy couch in her bedroom and there we talked. She shared her thoughts about spirit and spirituality—and how it moves and shapes her life; about service and grace and giving. She celebrated the spirit of our people and the earthy sensuality of the sisterhood; she talked about family, and discussed how some of us have gone astray and how we can move to regain our way. These are some of her lessons in living.

Spirit

When I think of spirit, I think of the energy of life. African religions encourage the supplicant to respect the spirit in the tree, in the water, in the flower, in the air, in a child. I, too, am aware of the presence of spirit in everything. And because I am a religious woman, I cannot—don't know how to and don't wish to—separate spirit from the spirit of God. So spirit to me is God.

Last night a friend asked me how I dealt with depression. My answer was that when I find myself depressed, I ask the spirits to fill me. I say I am willing, I need you. And so I become—and this is where spirit and religion intersect—enthused. Now, if you look up the word enthusiasm or enthused, the root meaning is in fill—God in you. So what seems to be a kind of vibrancy in me is from having called on spirit, having called on God to fill me, and then: I'm enthusiastic! I'm up! I'm doing! I'm believing! I'm trying! I'm failing! I'm losing! I'm finding! It's all all right, you see.

I have tried many things, failed at many, and succeeded at many. I will try anything that I think is good, because I find myself surrounded by spirits in front of me, behind me, under me and over me. Spirit fills me. And it never leaves me. Now mind you, I may be silly enough to leave it for a while, but it never truly leaves me. All I or any of us need ever do is call.

My grandmother, who was one of the greatest human beings I've ever known, used to say, "I am a child of God and I'm nobody's creature." That to me defined the Black woman, through the centuries.

But something has happened that's been really disastrous for our people. We became enchanted with the attitudes, the postures, the material things and the faithlessness of the larger society. And we gave up our birthright for a mess of pottage. We thought that in order to be sophisticated we had to become nonbelievers; that to show we were on par with the whites, we had to become atheists as demonstration of how really sophisticated we were.

Now, it is said by some of the great thinkers that the epitome of sophistication is to strive for simplicity, to run the gamut through all the affectations and return to utter simplicity. That is where our people were coming out of slavery—they had run the gamut and they were back at a place of sturdy, solid, reliable sophistication.

Our ability to have and to live on faith brought us through conditions more horrific than we can even imagine. Whenever I get out of touch with my power, I think of our people, in their chains, having no names, not being able to move one inch without the license of someone who purportedly owned them. And I think of the song these same people wrote—"I'm going to run on, see what the end is going to be." My God, what a people! I think of the people who wrote and sang, "If the Lord wants somebody, here am I. Send me;" And I am overwhelmed by the grace and persistence of my people.

Grace

Grace has to do with one's deliberate, chosen way of being in this world. The old cliché about seeing a glass of water with a certain amount of water in it and deciding whether it's half-empty or half-full is evidence of how one wants to see the world. And how one wants to see oneself in the world.

For a Black woman, the choice is imperative because the larger society, and quite often Black men and women, see her in a negative light. This so threatens her being that unless she determines who she is and how she sees herself, she will die. She will die daily. She will die hourly unless she chooses how she will see herself and her way of being in this world. This is the kind of liberation that is a harbinger of grace. When you are liberated, you are free to accept grace, to ask for it, to host it.

So when she decides I am first a gift—I am the creation of the Creator, and the Creator makes no mistakes, I belong to myself, I live inside this place, it is all of me that lives inside this place, and everything about me belongs to me first—the moment that decision is made, grace enters.

And being a host to grace provides one with gentility, a generosity, a spirit of forgiveness and humor. The minute you host grace, you speak slower, because you want to be understood. You speak more softly because you don't want to jar, offend or run anybody away (except those who mean you no good). Your gestures are larger, more open, more generous. You're less afraid because the external threat does not reach you quite so directly. Other people's ideas of you become much, much less important. And you literally do become more beautiful.

Sensuality

A part of Black women's spirituality has to do with their sensuality. We love the aromas of things. We really love pretty colors and they love us.

We really love food. Love to prepare it. Love to serve it, and love to eat it. We really love music. Love to hear it, love to make it, and make some of the prettiest music ever heard by the human ear. We really love sex. Love to enjoy it, love to give it. We do. We are sensual people and do not or deny it unless we are sick.

Our spirituality is fed by our sensuality—meaning that we are present in the world. That's what sensuality really means. It means I am present. I'm not over there somewhere. I am present in my own world. I admit to aroma. I admit to feeling. I admit to hunger. I admit to thirst. I admit to my need for sex. I admit I am present in my world.

Ofttimes when you remember being sent out of the room when Mama and her sisters were talking, you'd hear them almost burst with laughter. Quite often, what they have said is something very bawdy. Now, a lot of people don't realize how nice Black ladies talk, but that kind of humor is part of our sensuality. And I include everybody I know. People with whom I spoke yesterday. Ladies of an age and a stature who, when we talk, having spoken about the children, discussed what can I possibly do about this raging violence, what can I do about raging racism, what can I do? What can I do? After having encouraged each other, say, "You've gotten any? Girl, look here. Well, what's happening? Honey, listen. Let me tell you what happened to me last month." That's right. It's very important. And after one of those conversations, you feel like you've had a Jacuzzi and a massage and everything.

Friendship

I could never make it, I would never have made it without my sister-friends. I kind of gauge a sister-friend this way: If I had to be in a room with a lion, would this person come in there with me? Now, I probably wouldn't send for them because after they helped me vanquish the lion, I would have to deal with them asking, "What the hell were you doing there in the room with the lion in the first place?"

Oh yes, that bond is part of our strength, it helped us endure. It was forged in Africa, and strengthened during slavery. If we lose this love and self-respect and respect for each other, this is how we will finally die.

I have a new poem which is too hot on that—"When will I stop and see that war is being waged on me?"

We see our men in prison, on drugs. The war is being waged against us. The final blow will be when we women are separated from each other.

Healing

It's scary to speak of the presence of evil in the world, but it's here. It may be that these two powers—god and the devil, the power of good and the power of evil—have been at each other beyond any concept of time. And I believe this evil is real in this world today because I see the proliferation of abuse: the rape; the abuse of children; the serial murderer, and then the horrific types of serial murderers. All of this speaks to something that somebody had better admit to, and very soon, and claim because as Bob Dylan wrote in one of his songs, "You got to serve somebody."

I think the first step is for those of us who have positions of power, which means of course the leaders, the teachers, the business people, the writers, the artists, the parents, aunts, uncles and cousins, all of us have got to take time out and look at where we are. That's the most important thing—to see and admit where we are. We don't have to admit it to anybody else, but to our individual selves.

Everybody ought to take a day off, not just from the job, but from family, friends, from everything, and sit down and think. Now that takes courage, because the world is moving so fast and our plates are overflowing with the things we got to do. But what we really have to do is take a day and sit down and think.

The world is not going to end or fall apart. Jobs won't be lost. Kids will not run crazy in one day. Lovers won't stop speaking to you. Husbands or wives are not just going to disappear. Just take that one day and think; don't read, don't write. No television, no radio, no distractions. Sit down and think. If you can't get everybody out of the house, go sit in a church, or the park, or take a long walk and think.

Call it a healing day. Just take a day to heal from all the lies you've told yourself and that have been told to you. And sometime during that day, admit where we are. Black women need to take that day of healing. But Black men must do the same if we are to survive. If women heal, but men do not, we will not survive intact. But if Black men also take that day of healing and admit who they are, and where we are, and try to figure out what to do, we might reverse this trend. Unless Black men do it, and we must expect them to, we will not survive, so we cannot afford to excuse them, or allow them to excuse themselves. We all need to take a day.

Giving

Giving is so fabulous, that is why the Christian Bible says it's more blessed to give than to receive, and why it's so true. Just give, not indiscriminately, but give. You'd be surprised how much unexpected laughter and glee and humor and wit enter one's life.

You know, a nurturing group of people like Black women, we don't volunteer enough. We ought to find some way at least twice a month to go to an old folks' home and read to somebody. Go into the children's ward. Go in there and read a children's story. Go, do something. Go to church and say, "I'm going to have about four hours every other Saturday, can you use me?"

Everybody needs to be needed. And it's not make-work; the truth is everybody is needed. And in giving you're healing at the same time, and being healed. Anybody who can't be used is useless. This does not mean the person should be abused or misused or overused or ill-used. But to be of use, to serve people in your state—what on earth are you here for if not for that? I feel for people who are not needed; it's terrible.

We make a terrible mistake if we think we are doing service for others. That is a mistake. We do service for ourselves. When you volunteer to do something for the community, it is important that you understand you're doing it for yourself. Yes, the people will benefit, and you will benefit more if you know I'm doing this for me. I am healing myself.

When you open a door, you hold it open because someone is going through it, because it's right to do. You want a "thank you." I do. But if the person doesn't say anything, I still say, "You're welcome." And if the same person came back through, I would hold the door again, because I'm doing it for myself, and it's the right thing to do for me.

Family

We have got to offer the spirit back to the children. If we don't we'll be dead. There's no question. We're well on our way to being out of here.

I was on this movie set in California and there was a young man cussing in front of everybody. He got into a big row with another young man, and they were going for each other's throat. One man came up and got between them. And the one who had started the trouble, he's still just cussing. I went over and I said, "Baby, may I speak to you for a minute?" He dropped his head, and I said, "Come on, let's walk."

And I started talking to him and started crying. I said, "Do you know how much at risk you are? Do you know how valuable you are to us? You're all we've got, baby."

He started crying, and said to me, "Don't cry." I don't know who has cried for him. And let him see how much he means, not accusingly, just "Darling, I love you so much. I'm going to tell you when you're wrong."

Bring the children into the life you live, and let them see you cry. Whatever they are, they're your children. They really don't want to see mother cry.

Too often we stem the tears and won't let them see us cry. We'd rather they see us shout and argue and slam doors. But let them see you cry. Explain to them, "Darling, my heart is broken and I'm worried to death. Now, I don't know where we're going from here, but I want you to know that you are my heart. You are all I have. You're the best I have. There's nobody better than you, and my heart is hurting now."

Let them see you cry. You don't have to accuse them of anything. Often what's needed is allowing your children, who are so vulnerable, to see that you are vulnerable, too. You will be surprised by how they respond to that because they always think that mother is so powerful. It's very important not to be such a superwoman as a mother that you don't have super children. You got to give to them. Let them be super-duper. Lean. Don't be ashamed of leaning.

What I do with my son, my grandson and three women I consider my daughters is put myself in their hands. I say, "I'm yours. Whatever you do will affect me. I am yours. I'm yours."

Now, I look after them. They're under my umbrella, but I don't take all of it. I say, "You take half. Look after me. I need you desperately. If you don't look after me, who will?" They begin to grow umbrellas so that their children will have something to stand under. And their friends, and I.

Black people say when you get, give; when you learn, teach. As soon as that healing takes place, then we have to go out and heal somebody, and pass on the idea of a healing day—so that somebody else gets it and passes it on. Upon admitting that we're about to go over the hill, about to slip down the crevice, one must stop and consider, admit and then heal. Takes a lot of courage to heal.

Each person must find her or his own mode of healing in the family. And bear in mind that true healing cannot come at someone else's expense. You have to be healthy. You have to develop the desire for health so deeply that you can liberate other people.

To get there you have to lay claim to your spirit. To those who would try to diminish me, I say you cannot cripple my spirit. You cannot do that, it is not yours to cripple. I alone am responsible to my God for my spirit. Not you, unless I give it to you. And I would be a fool. That is all I've got. I don't have my life. An airplane could fall down on me in this house, this minute. I don't have my health; in a blink of an eye, I could have a stroke. I don't have anything. The house can burn up, the telephone can ring, and I can be told my son and grandson have gone. I have nothing but my spirit, and I will not allow anyone to have or trample on it.

ONITA ESTES-HICKS

The Way We Were: Precious Memories
of the Black Segregated South

Following its publication in 1945, Richard Wright's immortal *Black Boy* served for decades as a paradigm for Black South autobiography. Closely allied to the slave narrative in content and in structure, Wright's masterpiece, like Douglass's classic narrative of his bondage and freedom, focuses on the "fortunate fall" of his younger self, whose precociousness and innate sense of dignity rendered him unfit for the unfreedom of the segregated South. The tale of the South recorded in "Richard Wright's Blues," as Ellison has accurately described *Black Boy*, depicted that region's unrelenting repression, a virtual war against Wright's humanity, eventuating in the author's decision to go north (*Shadow and Act* 89). Wright did not characterize his transit as a migrant's volunteer search for a better territory ahead, but as a refugee's forced flight for physical and psychological survival. A form of death-in-life, Wright's escape from the South presaged a new birth, an agonizing process of experiencing a self suppressed by social constraints and alienated by fear. Fingering that ragged grain of social death and self-alienation, Wright lamented:

> Not only had the southern whites not known me, but, more important still, as I had lived in the South I had not had the chance to learn who I was. The pressure of southern living kept me from

African American Review, Volume 27, Number 1 (Spring 1993): pp. 9–18. © 1993 Onita Estes-Hicks.

being the kind of person that I might have been. I had been what my surroundings had demanded, what my family—conforming to the dictates of the whites above them—had exacted of me, and what the whites had said that I must be. Never being fully able to be myself, I had slowly learned that the South could recognize but a part of a man, could accept but a fragment of his personality, and all the rest—the best and deepest things of heart and mind—were tossed away in blind ignorance and hate. (227–228)

Like the classic slave narrative, *Black Boy* concludes with its brutalized hero bound for safer ground in the North, its immemorial lyricism anticipating relief from the harsh conditions of oppression in the Black South:

I was leaving the South to fling myself into the unknown, to meet other situations that would perhaps elicit from me other responses. And if I could meet enough of a different life, then, perhaps, gradually and slowly I might learn who I was, what I might be. (228)

As their titles sometimes reflect, post-*Black Boy* autobiographical writings by refugees from the Black South continued to bemoan the homeland as wasteland and as enemy territory. Fashioned in the bondage-freedom structure which Sidonie Smith has discerned at work in the African American autobiographical tradition, these texts also stressed the necessity of flight from the feared fatherland—featuring their authors as homeless in the native land, on the lam for life and limb. Writings by Joe Loids (*My Life Story*, 1947), Walter White (*A Man Called White*, 1948), William Lee Broonzy (*Big Bill's Blues*, 1955), Ellen Tarry (*The Third Door*, 1955), Eartha Kitt (*Thursday's Child*, 1956), Richard Robert Wright (*87 Years Behind the Black Curtain*, 1965), and H. Rap Brown (*Die Nigger Die*, 1969) not only echoed the "trauntatic experience" of oppression voiced by Wright (Fabre xviii), but also retraced the refugees' confrontation with the South's "white terror" (Fabre 52), which necessitated dramatic flight from Black South communities in Alabama, Georgia, North Carolina, Mississippi, South Carolina, and Louisiana.

Years after he was forced to abandon his native Tennessee for safety and opportunities above the Mason-Dixie line, Carl Rowan in the autobiographical essays contained in *Go South to Sorrow* (1952) and *South of Freedom* (1957) discussed a hostile and static South whose regime of repression alienated him from the land of his birth. Writing of having broken "all mental ties with [his] hometown" in 1943 (*South* 3), Rowan in his 1991 autobiography evoked another Wrightian resonance; he begins *Breaking Barriers* with a rat-chasing scene which bears acute resemblances to the opening pages of *Native Son,* which itself evidences aspects of Wright's own history.

Marked by a pattern of bondage-flight-freedom, these deeply moving autobiographical reflections by native sons and native daughters of the South conceded the irrevocable loss of the land of nativity, accepting flight and natal alienation as the necessary terms for survival and success in surrogate homelands.

A product of the third period of African American autobiography (Butterfield), and building upon first and second-period paradigms classically represented by Douglass and Wright respectively, Maya Angelou's *I Know Why the Caged Bird Sings* (1970) inaugurated a new phase of reminiscences about experiences in the Black South. Faithfully and fatefully portraying the horrors of the old, apartheid South, the dominant theme of earlier black autobiography, Angelou's record of her formative years in Stamps, Arkansas, backgrounded a positive vision of an autonomous black community centered in the economic independence of Mrs. Annie Henderson, the author's resilient paternal grandmother. Parallelled in other "third-period" autobiographical writings of the seventies, Angelou's autobiographical mode, while foregrounding the South as what Baraka has characterized as "the scene of the crime" (95), imparts an emerging yet tentative measure of acceptance of the once reviled region. Autobiographical essays, statements, and poems by Alice Walker; the account of coming of age in Mississippi left by Anne Moody; and the "tortured-tenth" introspection of Leslie Lacy were to constitute a new departure in ways of looking at the South.

Reflecting both social and literary change, more recent soul-searching of the self shaped by the segregated South heralds an important "fourth phase" of Black South autobiography. Represented by Clifton Taulbert's *Once Upon a Time When We Were Colored* (1989), Raymond Andrews's *The Last Radio Baby: A Memoir* (1990), and Dorothy Spruill Reciford's *Somerset Homecoming: Recovering a Lost Heritage* (1988), this new mood and mode of return and reconciliation foregrounds reconciliation with the Southern past.

Maya Angelou, in her popular *I Know Why the Caged Bird Sings,* attributes her youthful departure from the South, which served as home to her and her beloved brother Bailey, to their wise grandmother's concern for Bailey's safety after a local white forced Angelou's fourteen-year-old sibling to assist in disposing of the body of a "dead and rotten" black male (192). While documenting the "forced-flight" pattern of earlier Black South autobiographies and acknowledging the "burden of impotent pain" which Jean Toomer so movingly captured in his autobiographical *Cane,* Angelou was to pay homage to that soulful beauty which Toomer himself had found in the old apartheid South during his brief, 1922 sojourn in Sparta, Georgia. Joanne Braxton's study *Black Women Writing Autobiography* calls attention to *Caged*

Bird's radiant remembrances of things past in Stamps, Arkansas, tracing Angelou's vision of nurturing family and cohesive community to post-generic
influences in the genre of autobiography.

Punctuated by life-sustaining community rituals involving church gath-
erings, storytelling sessions in the family-owned store, and cooperative work
projects (such as annual hog slaughterings, preserving and canning activities,
and work in the cotton fields), Angelou's poignant portraits of her immediate
family's orderly daily life suggest some measure of the stability which graced
the lives of Black Southerners based on the mutual need, reciprocal respect,
and shared compassion which oppression encouraged. Maya's grandmother's
store, "the lay center of activities in town" (7), gave the writer a Hurston-like
post from which to observe the rich life of small-town Arkansas in the thir-
ties during her ten-year stay in the South:

> In those tender mornings the Store was full of laughing, joking,
> boasting and bragging. One man was going to pick two hundred
> pounds of cotton, and another three hundred. Even the children
> were promising to bring home fo' bits and six bits. (9)

Profoundly aware of the history of forced flight from countless cruel cradles
of the confederacy, Alice Walker has sadly and bitterly written of the pain
caused by exodus from the Southern landscape. In a 1972 address delivered
in a newly desegregated, formerly "for white's only" restaurant, the Georgian
declared:

> I watched my brother's, one by one, leave our home and leave the
> South. I watched my sisters do the same. This was not unusual;
> abandonment, except for memories, was the common thing, except
> for those who could not do any better," or those whose strength or
> stubbornness was so colossal they took the risk that others could
> not bear. (*In Search* 143)

Walker, too, has recalled not only the pain but also the beauty and the
bounty of the Black South, which she has nostalgically evoked in lingering
and loving memories of her childhood in Georgia.

Steeped in the lyrical reverie of a reluctant refugee's repository of precious memories, Walker's autobiographical essays resonate with that devotion
to the Georgia terrain which Toomer had earlier bequeathed to the forthcoming "genius of the South" (*Cane* 22). "I am nostalgic for the land of my
birth," Walker has confessed, "the land I left forever when I was 13—moving
first to the town of Eatonton, Georgia, and then, at 17, to the city of Atlanta"
(*Her Blue* 412). Walker identifies herself as a relative of Brer Rabbit, a fellow

Georgian, dispossessed of her briar patch, "overlooking another world" from her home in California but looking back to Southern roots:

> I remember early morning fogs in Georgia, not so dramatic as California ones, but magical too because out of the Southern fog of memory tramps my dark father, smiling and large, glowing with rootedness, and talking of hound dogs, biscuits and coons. And my equally rooted mother bustles around the corner of our house preparing to start a wash, the fire under the black wash pot extending a circle of warmth in which I, a grave-eyed child, stand. There is my sister Ruth, beautiful to me and dressed elegantly for high school in gray felt skirt and rhinestone brooch, hurrying up the road to catch the yellow school bus which glows like a large glow worm in the early morning fog. (*Her Blue* 413)

Adumbrated in poetic stanzas of "My Heart Has Returned to You," an autobiographical poem prefaced by the above excerpt in her 1991 collection of "earthling poems," Walker's recollections of the place where she was born register the murmurings of a "stricken heart" faithful to its

> "earliest love," to which it has reopened and returned:
> O, landscape of my birth because you were so good to me as
> I grew I could not bear to lose you.
> O, landscape of my birth because when I lost you, a part of
> my soul died.
> O, landscape of my birth because to save myself I pretended
> it was you who died. You that now did not exist because I could
> not see you.
> But O, landscape of my birth now I can confess how I have lied.
> Now I can confess the sorrow of my heart as the tears flow and I
> see again with memory's
> bright eye my dearest companion cut down and can bear to resee
> myself so lonely and so small there in the sunny meadows and
> shaded woods of childhood where my crushed spirit
> and stricken heart
> ran in circles
> looking for a friend. (414)

Her analytical skills as acute as her aesthetic sensibilities, Walker had earlier attributed the change in her Southern perspective to transformations in the social fabric of the South, tracing those now historical adjustments to the incomparable leadership and love which Martin Luther King, Jr., brought to the modern freedom struggle waged on once-wretched Southern soil: "It was Martin, more than anyone who exposed the hidden beauty of black people in the South, and caused us to look again at the land our fathers and mothers knew" (*In Search* 156). Imbuing his followers with deep faith in their own abilities to reclaim Southern terrain, the ringing cadences of King's stirring 1963 "I Have a Dream" March-on-Washington speech counseled those brave Southern marchers who had come to Washington in their trust of Dr. King to "go back to Mississippi, go back to Alabama." Following Dr. King's carols of courage, they indeed went back to the daunting task of "opening the black south," participating in scores of home-based actions and activities which nourished new dimensions of freedom.

These struggles for the modern South in turn generated that very same acceptance of the South transmitted in post-civil rights autobiographies. Grateful for the opening of hotels, which historically had been closed to blacks, Walker, who also foresaw the possibility of healing which new forms of hospitality made possible, deeply understood the historical schism which closed housing had caused by severely limiting visits of relatives and friends of Black South residents.

Published in 1969, Anne Moody's stunning *Coming of Age in Mississippi*, is especially valuable for its depiction of the extraordinary spiritual bonds which existed in the segregated South and which emboldened long suppressed locals to make a stand for freedom. Covering Moody's life from age four through her graduation from Mississippi's Tougaloo College in 1964, Moody's narrative richly conveys the dense social network which protected Northern freedom riders and which sustained black Mississippians throughout the renewed reign of white terror in the sixties. Embraced by an extended family of civil rights participants and supporters, Moody worked out of a Freedom House in Canton, Mississippi, a deeply racist and vicious Old South small town whose blacks turned out in droves to support the Tougaloo students, in spite of the fact that "every hick in the county had been deputized" and they displayed "guns hanging off their hips like cowboys" (369). Returning to Canton for a mass rally, Moody also returned to the love and security of a family:

On Friday, May 29, 1964, I was again headed for Canton, Mississippi. When Dave drove up in front of the Freedom House, the first person I saw was Mrs. Chinn. I jumped out of the car before it came to a complete stop and ran to her. "Anne! Anne! Anne!" she kept saying as we hugged each other. A minute later, I was hugging Mrs. Devine, then George, and it went on and on from one to the other for about thirty minutes. (369)

By the time he wrote *The Rise and Fall of a Proper Negro,* in 1970, Leslie Alexander Lacy had himself come to terms with the segregated South of his birth, expressing this understanding in acceptance of his father, whose failure to protect his upper-middle-class family from the ravishes of racism, small-town Louisiana style, had alienated the young Lacy not only from Louisiana but also from his very proper father. His childhood and youth marked by exposure to Klanstyle killings and by observations of roguish whites' humiliating his dignified patriarch, Lacy, like Moody, Angelou, and Walker, foregrounds "forced-flight" themes. Yet his narrative also resembles theirs in its dormant, background portrayal of a comforting, close family steeped in a beloved community, even though classism restricted the Lacy family circle first to a small network in the little town of Franklin, then later to a more sizeable group encompassing the well-to-do black residents in the larger Northern Louisiana community of Shreveport. In contrast to the limited living space of small huts and hovels in most Black South autobiographies, Lacy's childhood residence provided ample space and prompted precious memories of an affluent past.

My first recollections of life are of a big comfortable house of white wood with front and back porches which in late spring and early summer were shaded with rosebushes. Spreading out eastward from the front was a beautiful street whose trees kept us dry during the spring rains. To the west was a spacious yard with a garden, two large doghouses for our German shepherds, and a large garage ... (19)

Nkrumah's Ghana, a stop on the author's quest for self-knowledge and for meaning of his life as an African American male, provided Lacy more distance from the segregated South and its ravishes than had an earlier stint at law school in San Francisco following his traumatic exposure to Boston College after graduating from the very proper African American preparatory school, Palmer Memorial Institute in Sedaba, North Carolina. Through the author's bittersweet and ambivalent focus on Palmer, there emerges the portrait of playful yet purposive youth that attests to the substantial nature of Black South existence inscribed in *The Rise and Fall of a Proper Negro.* Backed by affluent and ambitious parents, Palmer and other private preparatory academies and boarding schools as well as private colleges shaped students to take positions of leadership in the Black South.

Presaging the new direction of return and reconciliation in Black South autobiography Clifton L. Taulbert's 1989 book *Once Upon a Time When We Were Colored* lays claim to recapturing the culture and codes of the South in the author's transvaluation of the word colored, his reassessment of the region, and his rewriting of his black boyhood in that mean Mississippi Delta which shaped not only Wright's *Black Boy* but, by virtue of Wright's prodigious influence, also set the tone and texture for many Black South texts. Loosely structured in the leisurely mode of memoir, *Once Upon a Time* engages the author's once-problematic, poverty-ridden Southern past from the distance of his far different, highly developed self. In sympathy with the moral certainties shaped by his earlier material poverty, Taulbert "resees" the receding past of his restricted life in Glen Allen, Mississippi, with a deep appreciation of the uses of adversity, substituting tempered tolerance for Wrightian rage.

Demonstrating the self-selectivity and instrumentality of memory, Taulbert, who departed from his native land in 1963 at the age of seventeen for better opportunities, made a "yearly pilgrimage to see Glen Allen, Mississippi, to remember the life [he] once knew and visit [his] older relatives" (2). He felt compelled to write his memoirs after an aged relative passed on to him the records and deeds documenting that "once upon a time" his poor ancestors had possessed sizeable tracts of land, which, in classic Black South fashion, the family had lost through crafty collusion among the ubiquitous good old (white) boys whose greed and need controlled small towns in the South. Relegating the antics and outrages of the good old boys to the background of his narrative, Taulbert digs deep down into the crevices of "colored" community life in the old South, resurrecting the culture of the "colored colony" (3) which "had given [him] strength when [he] was a child" (2). The child of a single mother, the Mississippian centered his life on his maternal grandfather, a dignified "Black Budda of the South" (8). "Poppa" used his deft knowledge of the protocol of segregation to protect young Taulbert and scores of other members of Glen Allen's "colored colony," sheltering his young charge from "the harsher realities of our complex social environment" (11) and serving "as a go-between for the coloreds when problems arose involving whites" (10). Taulbert learned the codes of growing up colored and male under the loving tutelage of Poppa, inscribing male bonding rituals between boy and man, much as Angelou had depicted the female bonding which took place between girlchild and beloved grandmother. Writing of his highly anticipated weekly trip to a larger nearby town with his grandfather, the younger man captures both the rhythms of life with Poppa and the older man's meticulous grooming ritual:

> Impatient to go, I'd ease into the front room, where Poppa would be putting the finishing touches on his shaving. He shaved his face and head every day. There he'd sit in the big black leather parlor chair by the door to the small bedroom, sharpening his razor on the long razor strops hung by the door. I would watch in complete silence as the long blade of the razor, expertly handled, removed all signs of hair from his face and head. Afterwards Poppa would run alcohol all over his scalp with a hot towel, then he would rub oil over his face and head, creating the shiny image of a Black Buddha that I had come to love.

Thanks to Poppa's example, Taulbert grew up loving both the patriarch and that art of manly grooming which cultivated an appreciation for the aesthetics of ordinary life in the Black South, in spite of the region's poverty:

> With the shaving complete, I knew it wouldn't be long. Poppa would put on his best white shirt and black suit. He'd chain his gold pocket watch across his belly, then get his hat. While he was finishing this careful process of dressing, I sat on the tall steps that led to the front porch. (12)

Published in the "middle passage" of the author's life at age forty-three, Taulbert's text rings with worship of ancestors and elders. His book suffuses gratitude for past help given him by aged relatives and friends whose constant preachments "to do good in school" because "ain't nothing to field work" (14) were delivered with the poignant knowledge of preparing their beloved one to leave the area. Though living in a decrepit sharecropper's house, one old man always queried Taulbert about "what [he] wanted to be when [he] grew up" (13) and constantly encouraged the young boy that he could be anything [he] wanted to be" (14), advice Taulbert also received from the older women who constituted the "mothers" of the church which he attended. The author records the significance of the church and the amazing grace with which each Sunday redeemed the week and transformed fieldhands into a unified elect:

> It was Pastoral Sunday, and there was a great feeling of togetherness as we neared the church.

Women in their white dresses and black Sunday hats and men in their Sunday suits with their best brightly colored ties and shined shoes were shaking each other's hands, hugging and kissing the children as we took our turns climbing the steps into the main sanctuary. Today field hands were deacons, and maids were ushers, mothers of the church, or trustees. The church transformed the ordinary into an institution of social and economic significance. (94)

Once Upon a Time When We Were Colored describes secular communal rituals which brought healing to Taulbert's small town. The historical importance of Joe Louis is highlighted in Taulbert's text, and the vital vicarious existence which Louis's national prominence provided receives detailed presentation in Taulbert's narrative, as it does in the works of Angelou and Raymond Andrews. Gathering around the only radio in the black community to hear Louis's fights, residents shadowboxed, placed bets, breathlessly waited for countdowns, their "colored" and brown identities tied to the fortunes of the "Brown Bomber," whose fights with white opponents served displacement functions, became surrogate battles which released the community's pent-up aggression.

Transformed himself by years of returning to his native land, comparing different phases of his life in that "before-and-after" pattern which James Olney contends forms the dominant structure of autobiographical writings, Taulbert learned to love the land of his birth and came to grips with some of its false values which he had internalized. Realizing that the "slaving instinct" which drove the oppressive use of black labor has roots in the false consciousness that land and people can be owned, Taulbert receives a true measure of liberation from the wounds of growing up in the old segregated South when he challenges that region's fixation on land as the basis of self-worth:

> On further reflection, I realized that many of the values of the Southern culture had been illegitimate, even, perhaps, the value placed on land ownership. For the truth is, man cannot really own the land; we are only trustees for a time. Eventually the land will claim us and we'll return to our mother earth. Knowing this gives me some solace as I look at the antiquated deeds dated in the late 1800s and signed over to my great-great grandparents by the vice-president of the Yazoo and Mississippi Valley Railroad Company and its land commissioners. The land, once called Freemount, has probably had more trustees and names than we'll ever know.

Relinquishing the desire for ancestral land, Taulbert rescues precious memories that nurture reconciliation with the region of his beginning:

> If land ownership is not a legitimate measure of a people's worth, I wondered, what is? I began to think about my childhood and other values I'd learned as I grow up in an environment much like that experienced by thousands of other colored Americans. Even though segregation was a painful reality for us, there were some very good things that happened. Today, I enjoy the broader society in which I live and I would never want to return to forced segregation, but I also have a deeply-felt sense that important values were conveyed to me in my colored childhood, values we're in danger of losing in our integrated world. As a child, I was not only protected, but also nourished, encouraged, taught, and loved by people who, with no land, little money and few other resources, displayed the strength of a love which knew no measure. I have

come to believe that this love is the true value, the legitimate measure of a people's worth. (5)

Written from the same autobiographical perspective of return and reconciliation, by an author who returned and re-established residency in the South, Raymond Andrews's book *The Last Radio Baby: A Memoir* carries many of the same structural features discernible in Taulbert's text. Penned in that raucous and ribald humor which the author used in his earlier autobiographical novels about life in the Georgia Piedmont Region (*Appalachee Red, Rosiebelle Lee Wildcat Tennessee,* and *Baby Sweet's*), this dense look at the first fifteen years of life radiates the joy of growing up amid countless relatives and innumerable neighbors in the small black community of Plainview, Georgia. As does *Once Upon a Time When We Were Colored, The Last Radio Baby* presents the triumph of a family and a community over racist-ridden obstacles, showing the survival strategies which humanized the most lowly tasks. Paralleling Moody, Angelou, and Taulbert in describing methods the folk generated to cope with hard labor in the fields, Andrews writes of a "memorable event" which transpired during a peach-picking season when he was colored:

> The most memorable event of my years in the orchard occurred during my first peach-picking summer, 1945, in the orchards near Putnam County. One lunch hour appeared this very pretty young colored girl of about fifteen or sixteen years old to dance alone before—shortly—a large surrounding crowd of hand-clapping workers (sharecroppers and peachpickers side by side) beneath the hot sun there in the dusty big orchards. Following this introduction, each day she appeared at lunch to dance, sometimes alone and sometimes with males, one at a time, from the crowd. There was no music for her dancing, just hand-clapping, finger-popping, and humming from the always big crowd surrounding her. One day following her dance, while walking past on her way back into the orchards, she looked me right in the eye and smiled. Not just with her lips but with her eyes. I fell instantly, and madly, in love with her. (84)

The genealogical chronicle of Plainview rivals those found in the Old Testament, and, no doubt, the long list of neighbors and relatives provided young Andrews the same sense of belonging given to his Biblical counterparts. As the owners of the small community's first radio, the Andrews family hosted Plainview's "Joe Louis fight crowd," with Andrews's father "continually trying frantically to bring in the sound of the fight through the never-

ending noise of popping static coming through like rapid machine-gun fire
mixed with exploding shells" (34). *The Last Radio Baby* recalls the community
uproar after each Joe Louis victory:

> Daddy got better at announcing with each Joe Louis fight. But what
> I'll never forget about those fight nights was the big WHOOP!!!
> that went up from the crowd at our house and could be heard nearly
> all over Plainview when the referee, or Daddy, announced, "The
> winner and still champion, Joooo Looouisss!!!" (34)

Reveling in personality and place, Andrews's memoir of growing up
"colored" in Georgia in the 1930s and the 1940s nostalgically evokes the
same respect for elders and kin imparted in Taulbert's text and celebrates
some of the same codes captured by the Mississippian: weekly trips to town,
cotton-picking contests with the invariable boasting, songfests, departures
from the South on one-way tickets which signal "another thousand gone,"
and visits from Northern relatives whose seeming glamour and independent
behavior established new norms of aspiration for locals. Both authors write
of the flow of goods and services between Northern and Southern members
of their families: boxes of clothes from better-placed Northerners came in
exchange for homemade mementoes from the South (quilts, scarves) which
kept precious memories alive on Northern turf. These strenuous efforts to
retain bonds across long distances in those pre-telephone days, when arduous
travel on segregated Greyhound buses and trains provided the major forms of
travel, document the strength and cohesiveness of Black South families.

Likewise, Dorothy Spruill Redford's black family chronicle *Somerset
Homecoming: Recovering a Lost Heritage* represents a distinct achievement in
Black South autobiography. The story of her return to and reconciliation with
the South, *Somerset Homecoming* is also the record of Redford's reconstruction of her ancestral community in Washington County, North Carolina. In a
classic autobiographical rite, Redford retraces and reclaims the history of the
slaves of the Somerset Place plantation, an antebellum mansion built by her
ancestors. Assembling over 2,000 descendants of the Somerset plantation for
a homecoming in 1986, Redford's prodigious feat of at-home healing took
place in the restored Somerset mansion and anticipated restoration of the entire slave quarters as a national historic site depicting the life of slaves. A high
point of return and reconciliation, *Somerset Homecoming* records that form of
reclaiming the self which is the driving force of autobiography.

Discussing the ontology of autobiography, William Andrews states
in *To Tell a Free Story* that the "writing of autobiography is in some ways
uniquely self-liberating, the final climactic act in the drama of . . . the quest
for freedom" (xi). In its most recent phase of return and reconciliation, Black

South autobiography manifests the regaining of freedom on Southern soil, an act of transcendence which transforms the primal "scene of the crime" into a sanctuary of beloved community.

Works Cited

Andrews, Raymond. *The Last Radio Baby: A Memoir*. Atlanta: Peachtree, 1990.

Andrews, William. To *Tell a Free Story: The First Century of Afro-American Autobiography, 1760–1865*. Urbana: University of Illinois Press, 1986.

Angelou, Maya. *I Know Why the Caged Bird Sings*. New York: Random House, 1970.

Baraka, Amiri. *Blues People*. New York: Morrow, 1963.

Braxton, Joanne M. *Black Women Writing Autobiography: A Tradition within a Tradition*. Philadelphia: Temple University Press, 1989.

Broonzy, William Lee Conley. *Big Bill's Blues: William Broonzy's Story*. 1955. New York: Oak 1964.

Brown, H. Rap. *Die Nigger Die*. New York: Dial, 1969.

Butterfield, Stephen. *Black Autobiography*. Amherst: University of Massachusetts Press, 1974.

Ellison, Ralph. "Richard Wright's Blues." *Shadow and Act*. 1964. New York: NAL, 1966. 89–104.

Fabre, Michel. *The Unfinished Quest of Richard Wright*. Trans. Isabel Barzun. New York: Morrow, 1973.

Kitt, Eartha. *Thursday's Child*. New York: Duell, Sloan and Pearce, 1956.

Louis, Joe. *My Life Story*. New York: Duell, Sloan and Pearce, 1947.

Lacy, Leslie Alexander. *The Rise and Fall of a Proper Negro*. New York: Macmillan, 1970.

Olney, James. *Metaphors of Self*. Princeton: Princeton University Press, 1980.

Redford, Dorothy Spruill. *Somerset Homecoming: Recovering a Lost Heritage*. New York: Doubleday, 1988.

Rowan, Carl T. *Breaking Barriers*. Boston: Little Brown, 1991.

———. *Go South to Sorrow*. New York: Random, 1957.

———. *South of Freedom*. New York: Knopf, 1952.

Smith, Sidonie. *Where I'm Bound: Patterns of Slavery and Freedom in Black American Autobiography*. Westport: Greenwood, 1974.

Tarry, Ellen. *The Third Door: The Autobiography of an American Woman*. 1955. Birmingham: University of Alabama Press, 1992.

Taulbert, Clifton L. *Once Upon a Time When We Were Colored*. Tulsa: Council Oak, 1989.

Toomey, Jean. *Cane*. 1923. New York: Harper, 1969.

Walker, Alice. *Her Blue Body: Everything We Know; Earthling Poems 1965–1990*. New York: Harcourt, 1991.

———. *In Search of Our Mother's Gardens: Womanist Prose*. New York: Harcourt, 1983.

White, Walter. *A Man Called White: The Autobiography of Walter White*. New York: Viking, 1948.

Wright, Richard. *Black Boy: A Record of Childhood and Youth*. New York: Harper, 1945.

Wright, Richard Robert. *87 Years Behind the Black Curtain: An Autobiography*. Philadelphia: Rare, 1965.

CASSIE PREMO-STEELE

When the Difference Becomes Too Great: Images of the Self and Survival in a Postmodern World

W hile the chaos that rages in the "real world" seems to happen as a result of the failure of Modernity's promises of justice and equality for all, within academia many debates run on as if such promises were hopeless from the start. Abandon Modernity, the Postmodernists say, and revel in the openness to difference, the play of multiplicity, the deconstruction of the self. It is, above all, the deconstruction of the unified, autonomous, coherent self that is presented as the liberative alternative to the repressive order of the present-becoming-past in our postmodern world.

And yet even within this postmodern theoretical context, the question arises: how much difference can one self take? Do we abandon unity, autonomy, and coherence completely? And if we do, how then does the self function? What happens when the difference becomes too great?

I will pursue these questions by examining two contemporary postmodern theorists, Trinh T. Minh-ha and bell hooks. Feminist women of color—the first Asian-American, the second African-American—both theorists work out of a consciously postmodern context. And yet their theories of subjectivity are themselves very different. I will focus on the ideas of subjectivity presented in Trinh T. Minh-ha's "Difference: 'A Special Third World Women Issue;'" from 1989, and bell hooks's "The Politics of Radical Black Subjectivity" and "Postmodern Blackness" from 1993. Then,

Genre, Volume 16 (1995): pp. 183–191. © 1995 Cassie Premo-Steele.

in order to evaluate the two theories of subjectivity, I will show how they operate—or fail to operate—when applied to Maya Angelou's *I Know Why the Caged Bird Sings*. For it is in this narrative that we can trace a journey of a self—being made and unmade, making and remaking—when the difference becomes too great.

Trinh works from the poststructuralist insight that subjectivity is a result of the power/discourse web. The power/discourse web operates most forcefully through language, which in poststructuralist theory is a mechanism enabling both subjugation and subjectivity. In such theories, identity (which implies unity and sameness) is replaced with subjectivity (which implies both subjugation and being made a subject). As Trinh T. Minh-ha writes, "In trying to tell something, a woman is told, shredding herself into opaque words while her voice dissolves on the walls of silence" (79). Such an account of subjectivity arises out of a context of oppression and provides a way of opposition, a way to "work toward the unlearning of institutionalized language" (80). Further, such an account of subjectivity appears most pressing to those who live under diverse forms of overt oppression: "You who understand the dehumanization of forced removal-relocation-reeducation-redefinition, the humiliation of having to falsify your own reality, your voice—you know" (80).

But it is not only those who are overtly oppressed that Trinh's theory addresses. In her writing, the "you" who know unravel to reveal a multiplicity of subjects. At first, Trinh writes of the "I" as oppressor and the "you" as oppressed: "I will grant you autonomy" (80), which is the most common understanding of the relation of self and other, subject and object. In this context, " 'difference' is essentially 'division' . . . a tool of self-defense and conquest" (82). Next, Trinh refers to the subjects, "you and I" the oppressed together: "You and I might as well not walk into this trap (82). Together, "you and I" become "us," opposed to "them," "the master and/or his substitutes" (83). Later, the subject is divided against itself as it splits between the "i," the abject, and the "I," the abject become subject through the tools of language, which welds the abject to the subject to form "i/I" (86). This division occurs in the individual subject and in groups, as the "I-who-have-made-it" confronts the "You-who-cannot-make-it" (86).

Thus, for Trinh, the subject and the other are both multiply constructed in and through the other: "I/i can be I or i, you and me both involved" (90). Difference is "*both within* and *between* entities" such that "the natures of *I, i, you, s/he, We, we, they,* and *Wo/man* constantly overlap" (94). Thus, the subject is "not a unified subject. a fixed identity, or that solid mass covered with layers of superficialities one has gradually to peel off before one can see its true face" (94). The "I" is "infinite layers" (94). However, Trinh does not say what the infinite layers consist of, partly as a way to avoid a spatial metaphor which would privilege one layer over another, or perhaps in order to maintain consciousness throughout the layers. That is, consciousness for Trinh is not a unifying element, but constituted in and through disparate layers of construction.

Thus, the subject is not unified, not ruled by a unified consciousness, but produced by difference. "Difference as uniqueness or special identity is both limiting and deceiving" (95). That is, the subject is not different only from other unified subjects. The subject in its disunification holds difference within itself. It is through this reasoning that we come to speak of the "multiplicity of the subject."

Furthermore, multiplicity operates not only in the constitution of the individual subject, but multiplicity operates in the constitution of larger "subjects" such as communities and nations. "Third World has moved West (or North, depending on where the dividing line falls) and has expanded so as to include even the remote parts of the First World. What is at stake is not only the hegemony of Western cultures, but also their identities as unified cultures" (98). This has implications not only for "third world women," but for all of us. If there is not a clearly marked border between First and Third Worlds, between self and other, but if instead these identities exist together *within the borders* of the selves, nations, and worlds, then our conception of identity changes radically. As Trinh writes, "The master is bound to recognize that His Culture is not homogenous, as monolithic as he believed it to be. He discovers, with much reluctance, he is just an other among others" (98–99).

According to Trinh and other postmodern theorists, the possibility for liberation derives from this: "A thorough undermining of all power-based values would require the dismantling of the sovereign, authority-claiming subject, without which it is bound to be co-opted by power (103). It is at this point that the theory of subjectivity as multiplicity "slip slides" away to reveal what is ultimately unproductive. What values, I would ask, are not power-based? What are the criteria for determining such values? And where does this multiple, flowing, infinitely layered subject *stand* in deciding where to go once the dismantling is accomplished?

bell hooks attempts to answer these questions. As a contemporary theorist, she places her work within the context of postmodernism, drawing on its insights regarding the ways in which power systems work in the construction of our identities. She also continues the postmodern critique of essentialism, "while emphasizing 'the authority of experience.' There is a radical difference between a repudiation that there is a black 'essence' and recognition of the way black identity has been specifically constituted in the experience of exile and struggle" (29). Thus, bell hooks differs from what I would call the "pure postmodernists," such as Trinh T. Minh-ha, who focus on power only as repressive and liberation only as freedom from power.

hooks sees herself "on the outside of the discourse looking in" (24) and in doing so goes beyond postmodernism to envision action beyond opposition:

> How do we create an oppositional worldview, a consciousness, an identity, a standpoint that exists not only as that struggle which also opposes dehumanization but as that movement which enables creative, expansive self-actualization? Opposition is not enough. In that vacant space after one has resisted there is still the necessity to become—to make oneself anew. (15)

bell hooks uses spatial metaphors to present her theory of "radical black subjectivity." She begins by locating her self and her theory in a "marginal space of difference." By this she means the experience of being "outside" the dominant paradigms of self and discourse. Being outside the norms allows one to see the norm critically, according to hooks, and this leads to the development of a "critical consciousness." For hooks, consciousness is not fragmented as it is for Trinh; rather, it performs a unifying, a gathering, a "whole-making" function. It is precisely this "critical consciousness" that is missing in Trinh's account of subjectivity.

This "marginal space of difference" is also a place of great pain. When life and death depend upon your place in the spectrum of "normal," to live—and to try to survive—outside of that space, necessarily includes situations in which your difference causes you pain. It is the lived experience of this pain that hooks writes out of and through. In this way, she moves from the "real world" to text, theorizing in ways that may be helpful to those in such situations of painful lived experience. She distances her self from postmodernists who work only within textual realms where "subversive play happens much more easily . . . than in the world of human interaction . . . where repression is real" (22). As we will see in a reading of Maya Angelou's autobiography, hooks's theory of subjectivity functions best in contexts where "repression is real."

In such situations, being able to find a voice becomes crucial. Finding a voice implies having enough coherence and unity in the self in order to speak and act. Such coherence within the self is not desirable for Trinh T. Minh-ha, for it itself is an act of repression. The result of this, as we have seen in Trinh's writing, is a voice which is incoherent, twisted, and collapsing in upon itself. In hooks's writing, we see a recognition of difference balanced with a coherent voice. Throughout hooks's writing, her voice comes through clearly. In marked contrast to Trinh's writing, hooks's writing comes from the individual subject, "I," and the collective subject, "we." Never is the subject of hooks's writing an object, nor is it abject or passive. In the following, which serves as an example of the active subject that she uses in her writing, hooks describes the group to which she belongs, "writers, cultural critics, and artists who are poised on the margins" (19):

> We share . . . we critique . . . we are concerned . . . we are into . . . we
> see ourselves . . . we have no intention. . . . We all recognize. . . . We
> quote. . . . We are concerned. . . . We have a sense. . . . We believe.
> . . . We are concerned. . . . (19)

And while for Trinh difference operates not only between but within selves, so that subjects unravel in endless difference, for hooks there is the possibility of bridging the differences both within and between selves. hooks calls this possibility for connection "yearning."

> Yearning is the word that best describes a common psychological
> state shared by many of us, cutting across boundaries of race, class,
> gender, and sexual practice. Specifically, in relation to the post-
> modernist deconstruction of 'master' narratives, the yearning that
> wells in the hearts and minds of those whom such narratives have
> silenced is the longing for the critical voice. (27)

Thus, while yearning connects those who are different, it also allows for the possibility of questioning the terms of that difference. Recognizing our differences is possible due to the examination of issues of power, marginalization, and destabilization for which postmodern critique has paved the way. But, as hooks argues, simply recognizing our differences is not enough; we must find a way to use this recognition as a stepping stone toward a critique of domination. In order for this critique to take place, the subject must find her voice.

Maya Angelou's *I Know Why the Caged Bird Sings* is the autobiographical narrative of a black, female self coming of age within the contexts of communities to which she feels she both does and does not belong. Angelou's communities—the black communities of Stamps, Arkansas, St. Louis, Los Angeles, and San Francisco in the 1930's's and 40's—are also on the margins of the national community in this segregated era. As such, both the communities themselves and Angelou's place within those communities provide the "marginal space of difference" for the young Maya, then called Marguerite.

Trinh's analysis shows the power that differences have over and within subjects to shape the subject itself. As Trinh writes, "Difference does not annul identity. It is beyond and alongside identity" (104). Difference exists "alongside" identity in Angelou's narrative in many ways. As a child of divorced parents who is sent with her brother to live with their grandmother, she feels different from those in the small, rural community of Stamps, Arkansas, who more obviously "belong." Throughout her life, she will be "different" from those around her, and yet these differences will become a part of her identity, a sign of the complexity of who she is. In this way, Trinh's understanding of the multiplicity of identity-construction holds true in Angelou's narrative. However, there are instances when the difference becomes too great, where an external manifestation of power jams up against the subject in a way that is so painful that it cannot be easily integrated into the identity.

When we move from tracing the differences to showing the survival of the subject under differences that are more disruptive than constructive, we can see how hooks's conception of subjectivity is preferable over Trinh's for its ability to account for the subject's survival. By seeing how these disruptions are resolved in Angelou's narrative, we can see how she gains a voice, a coherence, rather than splintering into unresolvable fragments and hence losing her fight for survival. Ultimately, these moments of resolution, of finding a voice, lead Angelou to the development of a "critical consciousness," in which she goes from "being ignorant of being ignorant to being aware of being aware" (264).

The many differences—gender, class, race, nationality, and sexuality—in Angelou's narrative become too great many times. The difference of her gender is the first trauma that Angelou narrates, and the one I will focus on to illustrate what happens when the difference becomes too great. At age eight she is raped by her mother's boyfriend, Mr. Freeman. Angelou uses a Biblical metaphor to describe the rape: "The act of rape on an eight-year-old body is a matter of the needle giving because the camel can't. The child gives, because the body can, and the mind of the violator cannot" (76). This metaphor shows the spatial relation of the self to the other in times of painful difference. The young Marguerite tells her brother who raped her, and Mr. Freeman is arrested. In court, she lies and says that this is the first time such an act has happened. Soon after, Mr. Freeman is killed, set free from the guilt of survival, which leaves Marguerite to feel the full weight of her guilt:

> [A] man was dead because I lied. . . . Obviously I had forfeited my place in heaven forever, and I was as gutless as the doll I had ripped to pieces ages ago, Even Jesus Christ himself turned His back on Satan. Wouldn't he turn his back on me? I could feel the evilness flowing through my body and waiting, pent up, to rush off my tongue if I tried to open my mouth. I clamped my teeth shut, I'd hold it in. If it escaped, wouldn't it flood the world and all the innocent people? (84)

The eight-year-old displaces the guilt she feels about the rape onto herself, for believing that she is in control—to lie or not, to talk or not—is easier than accepting that she had absolutely no control in such a horrendous situation. It is at this point that she decides not to talk anymore. Her mother's family in St. Louis puts up with her "sullenness" for a while and then she and her brother are shipped back to their grandmother in Stamps, Arkansas. There her grandmother introduces her to Mrs. Flowers who, through love and books, urges her to speak again. As Mrs. Flowers tells her, "Words mean more than what is set down on paper. It takes the human voice to infuse them with shades of deeper meaning" (95). On this day, Marguerite speaks again for the first time in a year.

In many ways, the young Angelou confronts situations where the difference becomes too great and she must find a way to survive. When a white employer renames her "Mary," she rebels by coming late to work, doing poor work, and finally breaking the woman's prized dishes. When at her eighth grade graduation, the white speaker dashes the graduates' hopes of what they might become, the audience responds by singing the "Negro national anthem" (178). When her father takes her to Mexico and leaves her alone so that he can get drunk and be with a woman, she drives—for the first time in her life—him back to the border, taking the wheel of her life and her survival into her own hands: "As I twisted the steering wheel and forced the accelerator to the floor I was controlling Mexico, and might and aloneness and inexperienced youth and [my father] and death and insecurity, and even gravity" (232). And when she wonders about her own sexuality, she decides to find a boy to have sex with her, gets pregnant, keeps it to herself so she can finish school, and gives birth to a son.

In using her voice, resisting, singing, driving, and giving birth, Angelou shows readers the ways in which life-affirming action can arise out of painful situations. These actions enable her not only to survive, but to live critically, consciously. While Trinh T. Minh-ha's theory of subjectivity teaches that "difference" functions within and without the subject as a means of construction, this does not account for instances when the subject is confronted with differences that are too great. While the assumption underlies Trinh's essay that the subject either becomes complicitous or oppositional, Trinh gives no description of what enables a subject to choose. bell hooks's theory of subjectivity starts where Trinh's ends, showing how the subject has the ability to position herself in opposition to difference. Thus critical consciousness is born out of the marginal space where we find the ability to separate ourselves from that which threatens our survival. Critical consciousness is the ability to know that what threatens us is not what defines us. It is the ability to survive in the marginal space of difference when the difference becomes too great.

Works Cited

Angelou, Maya. *I Know Why the Caged Bird Sings.* New York: Random House,1969.

hooks, bell. "The Politics of Radical Black Subjectivity." In *Yearning: race, gender, and cultural politics.* Boston: South End Press,1990: 15–22.

———. "Postmodern Blackness." In *Yearning.* 23–31.

Minh-ha, Trinh T. "Difference: 'A Special Third World Women Issue,' " In *Woman, Native, Other.* Bloomington: Indiana University Press, 1989: 79–116.

DANA CHAMBLEE-CARPENTER

Searching for a Self in Maya Angelou's
I Know Why the Caged Bird Sings

In the postmodernist era, feminist and African-American activists and theorists struggle to answer questions about identity. What is a woman? What constitutes race? Is there some essential aspect of our nature that defines our gender and race, or are we a construct of society and language? Surprisingly, as these theorists debate the issues of identity on the grounds of established theory, biology, and innovative science, they seemingly ignore the plethora of written accounts of women and African-Americans investigating their own personal identities. Interestingly, these two groups have established a particular tradition in writing autobiographies for several reasons, not the least of which is an attempt to define their selves and develop a voice that might be heard in the white, male-dominated society and literary tradition. These autobiographies provide first-hand records of this quest for the self and explore the many avenues of and influences on the development of identity. Consequently, they provide a perfect location to examine the intricate theoretical issues of selfhood.

An analysis of Maya Angelou's autobiography, *I Know Why the Caged Bird Sings,* underscores the issues relevant to a young, African-American female's quest to know and develop her self. Angelou admits: "I decided many years ago to invent myself. I had obviously been invented by someone else—by a whole society—and I didn't like their invention" ("Maya" 88). In *Caged Bird,*

Publications of the Mississippi Philological Association (1996): pp. 6–12. © 1996 Dana Chamblee-Carpenter.

Maya Angelou, the adult poet and writer-subject, re-examines her "other" self, the self as it develops and begins to define its identity. As Eva Lennox Birch argues, this process of development "is painful, as one by one Angelou faces and has to overcome the constraints imposed upon her by her race and gender"(126–127). Within the autobiography, the young Maya becomes aware of the social norms that attempt to identify and label her. Society has already "invented" her, but rather than accept the reflections of her self seen in the eyes of the black community around her and the white society at large, Angelou defines her identity in spite of those social mirrorings.

Throughout the autobiography, Angelou is acutely aware of being looked at. In the opening prologue, a very young Angelou struggles to remember her lines at a church Easter presentation: " 'What are you looking at me for?/ I didn't come to stay . . .' " (1), and in a struggle to remember, she actually forgets lines, ultimately ending up with only " 'What are you looking at me for?' " (1) before urinating on herself and running out of the church in embarrassment. Angelou clearly establishes her discomfort at being looked at and, later, at being defined by the black community. Moreover, Angelou is also aware of the power of the white vision that consistently attempts to negate her race and gender. For instance, as Angelou anxiously awaits her eighth grade graduation, she is full of hopeful anticipation of the future—her promising future of infinite possibilities. However the white principal invited to speak at the graduation momentarily shatters her dreams: "The white kids were going to have a chance to become Galileos and Madame Curies and Edisons and Gaugins, and our boys (the girls weren't even in on it) would try to be Jesse Owenses and Joe Louises" (151). Angelou sees her self and her classmates in the reflection of the white man's vision. Her infinite possibilities unravel, and she sees a future of "maids and farmers, handymen and washerwomen, and anything higher that we aspired to was farcical and presumptuous" (152). Angelou actually loses her sense of identity in the aftermath of this whitewashing—"My name had lost its ring of familiarity and I had to be nudged to go and receive my diploma" (154). The mirror image revealed to her by the social norms mandated by white male society momentarily erases her identity. As in Lacan's mirror stage, the young Angelou acknowledges a self that is other, a self that is being looked at, a self defined by the black community and the white society.

These images are hardly "ideal," yet from the beginning, Angelou seems to have a sense of her self that challenges society's perceptions of her identity. Interestingly, Angelou's prologue focuses on the black community's inability to perceive the "true" Maya, as she imagines one day when all the people "were going to run up to [her] and say, 'Marguerite [sometimes it was 'dear Marguerite'], forgive us please, we didn't know who you were'" (2). They do not know her, but they think they do. They think she is like every other young, black girl. Moreover, they see only an external awkwardness that they define as ugliness—"I [Angelou] was described by our playmates as being shit color" (17) and "our elders said unkind things about my features" (17). In contrast to these reflections of her ugliness, the young Angelou imagines her self looking "like one of the sweet little white girls who everybody's dream of what was right with the world" (1). Although Angelou apparently succumbs initially to the powerful influence of the white vision, she also indicates that she has a sense of her self that not only challenges the actual reflection in the mirror, but also challenges the negative image of her self projected by the black community.

In her vision of her self, Angelou is not an ugly, awkward, black girl. Yet, as Birch suggests, "Blackness itself was no disbarment in Angelou's eyes to beauty. Her brother Bailey was lauded for his velvet black skin" (128). Additionally, for the young Angelou, the white community was something "to be dreaded" (20), and she "remember[s] never really believing that whites were really real" (20). Imagining herself to be white was less a *real* desire to be white, than it was a need for Angelou to feel beautiful. Unfortunately, little white girls did represent "what was right with the world," so the surest way of changing the perception of her self as ugly was to reinvent her self as white. Consequently, Angelou's anecdote simultaneously represents the struggle of a young black girl against the social norms of "what is right with the world" and her attempts to define her self in spite of the preconceived ideas about her identity reflected in the eyes of the black community.

Angelou's hazy fantasy about the non-people white folks quickly dissipates as she faces the real consequences of white dominated society. As previously indicated, Angelou becomes painfully aware of the negating power of that white society at her eighth grade graduation. Angelou cannot even find her reflection in the principal's version of the future, and she momentarily loses her sense of identity. However, Angelou eventually defines her self in spite of the white man's vision. After completing his "inspirational" address, the principal leaves, and a young black boy, the valedictorian of Angelou's class, leads the audience in the "Negro national anthem" which reinvigorates Angelou as she becomes "no longer simply a member of the proud graduating class of 1940; [she] was a proud member of the wonderful, beautiful Negro race" (156). She reinvents the future for her race and her self. Later, Angelou aggressively challenges the white principal's vision of her potential as she fights to become the first African-American conductor on the trolley in San Francisco: "I'd picture myself, dressed in a neat blue serge suit, my money changer swinging jauntily at my waist, and a cheery smile for the passengers" (225). When she learns that they do not accept African-American employees on the streetcars, Angelou refuses to allow the white world to disrupt her picture of her self as a conductor: "From disappointment, I gradually ascended the emotional ladder to haughty indignation, and finally to the state of stubbornness where the mind is locked like the jaws of an enraged bulldog" (225). Angelou recognizes the prejudice of the white vision that erases all sense of self—"the miserable little encounter had nothing to do with me, the *me of me*" (227 italics mine), and she even struggles with the "Negro organizations" (to which she appealed for assistance) whose officials "thought [her] mad" (227) for challenging tradition. Yet, Angelou determines to make them see her as a self, not a stereotype, and particularly, she makes them see her as *her* self, as a conductor on the streetcars.

However, although Angelou's autobiography functions much like Lacan's mirror, reflecting a sense of self as other, in the narrative, Angelou reflects that other self in terms of language. In the Lacanian mirror stage, the child has not yet acquired language, and consequently, he has not yet entered the symbolic order. Angelou's reflection of her self in her autobiography exists within that languaged symbolic order, and this further complicates her presentation of her developing identity. Although similar to Freud's version of the Oedipal cycle, in the Lacanian model, the phallus represents the real that was forfeited in order to gain access to the symbolic. As Silverman argues, this lack of the real initiates a system of desire in which the male wishes to obtain "the cultural privileges and positive values" (183) associated with the role of the father in the patriarchal society.

The female in the Lacanian model, as Silverman indicates, "neither succumbs to as complete an alienation from the real, nor enjoys as full an association with the symbolic" (186). Consequently, although both the male and female subjects in Lacan's model suffer from various lacks or separations, the female develops her identity based on a lack of lack. As Cixous argues, this effectively keeps the female "outside the Symbolic, that is outside language" (483), and consequently, "without man she would be indefinite, indefinable" (483). Because the female lacks the penis, she has no access to the phallus, consequently remaining connected to the real; but she also "acquires" language and so participates in the symbolic.

Whereas Lacan's male subject leaves the real for the symbolic, the female subject effectively splits to participate in both the real (phallus-less) and the symbolic (language). Moreover, as Catherine Belsey suggests, the female subject in the symbolic order splits once again to "participate both in the liberal-humanist discourse of freedom ... and at the same time in the specifically feminine discourse" (597–598). Although men also seemingly operate both as human and as man, they avoid a similar split in subjectivity because, as the dominant social force and fully situated in the symbolic, they mandate for themselves what it means to be human and man. Thus man and huMAN are synonymous. The female, however, must learn to define her self while functioning in the symbolic male discourse that has already defined her role as woman. The female subject is not simply huMAN. In Irigaray's words, "*She is neither one nor two*" (26), she is both. Consequently, the female in Lacan's model remains split. She remains aware of her self as other and of her self as real.

In *Caged Bird*, we can see the effect of the male symbolic on the black female self, and the clash of the symbolic and the real within that female self, through Angelou's representation of her self and the process of defining her identity. In particular, Angelou's reconstruction of her rape brutally expresses the violent aftermath of a wielded male power on the female body. Initially lured into the arms of Mr. Freeman (her mother's live-in lover) by the promise of tenderness and affection, a confused eight-year-old Maya misinterprets the molestation as the act of a true father. "From the way he was holding me I knew he'd never let me go or let anything bad ever happen to me. This was probably my real father and we had found each other at last" (61). However, months later, an older, more independent Maya no longer needs Mr. Freeman's "affections," so when he approaches her again, she rejects him: "I didn't need him to hold me anymore" (65). Mr. Freeman refuses to take no for an answer, and he rapes her:

> Then there was the pain. A breaking and entering when even the senses are torn apart. The act of rape on an eight-year-old body is a matter of the needle giving because the camel can't. The child gives, because the body can, and the mind of the violator cannot. (65)

Maya, the child, the body, the real, succumbs to the force of Mr. Freeman, the man, the symbolic; and in the aftermath, Angelou loses herself again—"My belly and behind were as heavy as cold iron, but it seemed my head had gone away and pure air had replaced it on my shoulders" (67).

Interestingly, Irigaray echoes the physical brutalities of rape to express what happens to a female self in a male society:

> This autoeroticism is disrupted by a violent break-in: the brutal separation of the two lips by a violating penis, an intrusion that distracts and deflects the woman from this "self caressing" she needs if she is not to incur the disappearance of her own pleasure in sexual relations. (24)

Just as Angelou "disappears" after Mr. Freeman "imposes" his own image of her as "Desire," the female self risks losing her sense of identity by necessarily functioning within the symbolic order dominated by a masculine discourse. In fact, as Cixous argues, many women escape from this torn self into silence or hysteria: "Silence: silence is the mark of hysteria. The great hysterics have lost speech. . . . They are decapitated, their tongues cut off. . . . In the end, the woman pushed to hysteria is the woman who disturbs" (486). Symbolically, Angelou loses her head after the rape, and she also loses her voice. Speaking only to her beloved brother Bailey, and then only out of necessity, Angelou remains mute for almost five years, and in her silence, she disturbs:

> When I refused to be the child they knew and accepted me to be, I was called impudent and my muteness sullenness.
>
>   For a while I was punished for being so uppity that I wouldn't speak; and then came the thrashings given by any relative who felt himself offended. (73)

For a time, Angelou retreats from the symbolic world of language, but Mrs. Flowers, a compassionate, African-American gentlewoman in the Stamps community, convinces Angelou that speaking is necessity. She coaxes Angelou back into the speaking world and thus back into the symbolic order.

   In order to disrupt the dominant male discourse, the female subject must position herself within the symbolic order, yet she also remains the other, still connected to the real and outside of that symbolic order. Often in *Caged Bird*, Angelou effectively disrupts the masculine discourse just as she challenges the image of her self reflected by society. In other words, not only does she reinvent her self, but she also reinterprets traditional male symbols as they apply to her own identity. For example, she refers to her vagina as her "pocketbook," heeding Momma Henderson's advice to "Keep your legs closed, and don't let nobody see your pocketbook" (61). Remembering this advice as Mr. Freeman molests her, Angelou maintains a sense of worth about her self and her sexuality. Irigaray describes the traditional view of the female sexual organ as " 'lack,' 'atrophy' and . . . the penis being the only sexual organ of recognized value" (23). Angelou challenges this traditional notion of the female sexual organ as a hole, a nothing, by implying that it contains some value as a pocketbook might hold money.

   Similarly, Angelou disrupts the most significant symbolic representation of woman in the male discourse when she challenges traditional notions of motherhood. Mary Jane Lupton suggests that Angelou's series of autobiographies focus "both literally and metaphorically [on] the significance of motherhood" (260). However, in *Caged Bird*, Angelou seems more driven by the *absence* of the mother-child contact, at least until the end when she becomes a mother herself. The narrative focuses entirely on Angelou's development as a young, African-American SELF, not her role as a daughter, or a granddaughter, or even as a mother. She reflects on her relationships with her mother and grandmother since they certainly affect her development as an individual. Yet even these relationships challenge traditional notions of mother and child. For example, as a young girl, Angelou has no recollection of her mother, so she creates a mental image to represent a symbolic Mother:

> I could cry anytime I wanted to by picturing my mother . . . lying in her coffin. Her hair, which was black, was spread out on a tiny little white pillow and her body was covered with a sheet. The face was brown, like a big O, and since I couldn't fill in the features I printed M O T H E R across the O, and tears would fall down my cheeks like warm milk. (43)

This hardly represents Lacan's vision of the ideal symbolic Mother, but it does indicate Angelou's representation of the ideal mother for her. Angelou's mother needed to be dead in order for Angelou to avoid feeling abandonment, and the melodramatic M O T H E R effectively erases any real sense of loss. Moreover, when Angelou eventually faces the terrifying moment of actually meeting her mother, her description still challenges any traditional concept of Mother—"To describe my mother would be to write about a hurricane in its perfect power . . . She was too beautiful to have children. I had never seen a woman as pretty as she who was called 'Mother' " (50). Throughout *Caged Bird*, Angelou depicts her mother as neglectful, beautiful but always absent. She left the eight-year-old Maya in the care of the man who would rape her, and then, unable to deal with the shattered and mute consequence, she again sends the children to the care of their grandmother.

Angelou's representation of her own motherhood at the close of the autobiography seemingly resembles the ideal symbolic mother. Although initially afraid of her new son, after her mother's coaxing, Angelou seems to accept that mothering comes naturally:

> But after closer investigation I found that I was lying on my stomach with my arm bent at a right angle. Under the tent of blanket, which was poled by my elbow and forearm, the baby slept touching my side.
>   Mother whispered, "See, you don't have to think about doing the right thing. If you're for the right thing, then you do it without thinking." (246)

This scene seems somewhat ironic when considering that the advice comes from Angelou's own mother who apparently was never "for the right thing" during Angelou's own childhood. Birch concurs that in Angelou's portrayal of her mother, she "was deliberately exploding another stereotypical myth: that motherhood in itself is completely fulfilling, that mother is a biological rather than a social function" (131). However, Birch argues that Angelou's "own life and love of her son deny this" (131). Interestingly, in the later autobiographies, Angelou frequently leaves her son with babysitters, seeing him only on weekends, and, reminiscent of her own childhood, Angelou also leaves him with her mother for several months in order to tour Europe with *Porgy and Bess*. Additionally, Angelou frequently comments in interviews that although she loves her son, she has "never been in love with him" ("Black" 63). Although Angelou certainly takes her role as a mother seriously, she also seems aware of maintaining her own separate sense of self, not an Angelou who is either all mother or just mother, and she challenges the traditional concept of an all consuming and forever nurturing motherhood.

In fact, in an interview, Angelou states, "To bring up a person healthily you have to be liberated. You have to be liberated from all sorts of things, for one, from being in love with the child" ("Black" 63). Throughout *Caged Bird*, Angelou liberates herself from the negative reflections of the black community and white society, and she challenges the restrictions of a male dominated symbolic order. In effect, Angelou liberates her self in order to "raise" a healthy concept of her self as a young, African-American female. She embodies the struggle of women to define their "selves" in a white, male-dominated society where definitions of identity pre-exist. Although Angelou's self in *I Know Why the Caged Bird Sings* is certainly in part a construction, it challenges any social or historical confines and becomes a construction of Angelou's own design.

Works Cited

Angelou, Maya. "The Black Scholar Interviews Maya Angelou." *Conversations with Maya Angelou*. Ed. Jeffrey Elliot. Jackson: University Press of Mississippi, 1989. 52–67.

———. *I Know Why the Caged Bird Sings*. New York: Bantam, 1969.

———. "Maya Angelou Raps." *Conversations with Maya Angelou*. Ed. Jeffrey Elliot. Jackson: University Press of Mississippi, 1989. 86–96.

Belsey, Catherine. "Constructing the Subject." *Feminisms*. Eds. Robyn Warhol and Diane Price Herndl. New Brunswick: Rutgers University Press, 1991. 593–609.

Birch, Eva Lennox. *Black American Women's Writing*. New York: Harvester, 1994.

Cixous, Helene. "Castration or Decapitation?" *Contemporary Literary Criticism*. Eds. Robert Con Davis and Ronald Schleifer. 2nd ed. New York: Longman, 1989. 479–491.

Irigaray, Luce. *This Sex Which Is Not One*. Ithaca: Cornell University Press, 1985.

Lupton, Mary Jane. "Singing the Black Mother: Maya Angelou and Autobiographical Continuity." *Black America Literature Forum* 24 (1990): 257–275.

Silverman, Kaja. *The Subject of Semiotics*. New York: Oxford University Press, 1983.

SIPHOKAZI KOYANA AND ROSEMARY GRAY

Growing Up with Maya Angelou and Sindiwe Magona: A Comparison

A comparison between Angelou's *I Know Why the Caged Bird Sings* (1969) and Magona's *To My Children's Children* (1990) reveals that the characters' journeys from childhood to untimely young motherhood have much in common, but ultimately bear an inverse relationship to each other. Their emerging sense of female selfhood is especially linked to cultural issues as well as the political structures in the USA and South Africa during the 1940s and 50s: namely civil rights, on the one hand, and apartheid, on the other. Broadly speaking, Angelou moves from anxious toddler to confident teenager, whereas Magona regresses from secure childhood to anxious youngster. Paradoxically, although black South Africans had a culture of their own, they had fewer opportunities in the dominant culture. By contrast, African-Americans (as a group) had, and have, greater access to active roles even though they are more dependent on the dominant culture. Not unnaturally, the extent of each group's access to opportunities depends on the constitutional rights or restrictions in each country, as is reflected, for example, in the elimination of school segregation in the United States (*Brown vs. Board of Education of Topeka*, 1954) at the time that it was enforced in South Africa (Bantu Education Act, 1955).

This distinction between the progressive American schooling system and the repressive South African one has a significant impact on the two

English in Africa, Volume 29, Number 1 (May 2002): pp. 85–98. © 2002 Siphokazi Koyana and Rosemary Gray.

young lives, producing an emergent consciousness of empowerment versus powerlessness; integration versus isolation; and identification or acculturation versus alienation. The autobiographies consequently reveal how these two writers use their experiences of growing up to explore the ways in which race, class, and gender effect and affect identity formation for those denied political representation. It emerges that the possibilities embedded in democracy outweigh the constraints inherent in the preservation of group identity in a manner that has a direct bearing on becoming a mother. As Isabel Hofmeyr notes: "We spend our years as a tale that is told."[1]

The autobiographical mode permits both writers to objectify the pain of their selected experiences, and in this article, the childhood self of memory is distinguished from the authors per se by the use of their given or first names for their 'characters.'[2] Magona insists on the authenticity of childhood memory but perhaps calls this assertion into question by invoking her remembered perception of being black by reminiscing on the childish game of make-believe:

> Perhaps children in other countries played at being kings and queens; we just played at being white.
> What I heard and what I saw were what I heard and what I saw.
> (*Children's Children* 40)
> I was a child and saw with the eyes of a child.

Here the poignancy of the comparison of playing 'at being white' rather than at being royalty clearly suggests a retrospective maturity in Magona's consciousness of a wider world than her own. Angelou's childhood consciousness is likewise conditioned by the sense of otherness but is arguably more authentically childlike, generated as it is by her excruciating sense of her own ugliness simply because she is not white. This emanates from her awareness of her physical dissimilarity to the doll-like, blond, white child-icon Shirley Temple. Her negative self-image is so strong that she imagines her misfortune of being born black (in 1928) as a "black ugly dream" from which she hopes one day to awake (*Caged Bird* 2). This negativity is intensified by parental rejection: at three, she is packed off with her four-year-old brother to Arkansas by incompatible parents. Her sense of loss and emotional displacement, common among children of parents undergoing divorce, is amplified not only by the geographical relocation by train but also by the fact that neither of the parents communicates with the children for the next three years.

However, there are two 'pillars' on which Maya leans in these lonely early years: the unwavering protection of Momma (Maya's paternal grandmother and the only black storekeeper and property owner in Stamps) and the companionship of her brother, Bailey. Momma, whose world is "bordered on all sides with work, duty, religion and 'her place'" (57), provides her grand-daughter with stability and a positive model of black female empowerment. As an active and devout member of her church, Momma introduces Maya to Christianity and its values as a mechanism for spiritual survival and political advancement, a role religion has played throughout the history of blacks in America.[3]

In contrast to the disruption of Christianity in Sindiwe's traditional religion (discussed briefly later in this paper), Christianity is liberating for Maya. The church is one of the few institutions where the black community can congregate without fear. In short, the role that Momma plays in anchoring Maya's life attests to both the strength of belief (faith) and black solidarity. Even though economic displacement often compels biological parents to live without their children, in America as in South Africa, "the grandmother can be counted upon to provide physical protection and spiritual nourishment, to perpetuate family history, and to retain and transmit moral values for the children" (Hill-Lubin 258). These strong bonds of the extended family as well as the adaptability of family roles within such structures are among the characteristics that have fostered the survival of black families and bereft individuals within those families.

In addition to the somewhat rigid impact of Momma's guardianship, the church and school, it is Bailey's brotherly support that makes it possible for Maya to salvage what little is left of her childhood innocence. He shares her pain of abandonment and helps her cope.[4] As a helping witness, who loves her without feeling the responsibility for raising her,[5] Bailey uses his adventurous spirit, his playfulness and sense of humour, his brilliance and love of books, as well as his protectiveness towards Maya, to create a cocoon which helps to shelter her fragile spirit. In the absence of parental love, however, Maya's faith in her brother approaches near-sacrilegious proportions. Of her belief in him, Angelou writes: "Of all the needs (there are none imaginary) a lonely child has, the one that must be satisfied, if there is going to be hope and a hope of wholeness, is the unshaking [sic] need for an unshakable God. My pretty Black brother was my Kingdom Come" (23).

Thus, the twin pillars of Momma and Bailey enable Maya to create order out of the all but overwhelming chaos in her young life. The intrusion of both parents, however, quickly snaps these supports. At six, Maya receives Christmas gifts from them. Her father later delivers her to her mother in California and her "seven-year-old world humpty-dumptied, never to be put back together again" (54). Maya's inability to respond to her mother emotionally, when she finally moves in with Vivian, is one of the saddest features of her childhood. Assailed by this stranger's beauty, the child handles this estrangement by turning inward, blaming her own imagined 'handicap.' In her eyes she lacks the beauty that she, her mother, and American society value so highly.[6] Maya's only solace is her mother's beauty, although this is poor consolation for an absence of maternal affection. Yet, it is precisely this reluctance to reject, judge, or condemn Vivian's violent, fast-paced, daredevil lifestyle that facilitates their later reconciliation after Maya produces a son.

This reconciliation is surprising and even ironic as the decisive trauma in the eight-year-old Maya's life was rape by Mr. Freeman, Vivian's live-in boyfriend. Rape underscores both the helplessness of children and the gendered nature of that helplessness. As a girl child, Maya is much more vulnerable to sexual molestation than her brother. The enormity of the trauma, perpetrated by one she had looked upon as a father figure, coupled with the pain of penetration, threats of violence and the rapist's subsequent death, not surprisingly prove more than Maya can handle; and six bleak years of autistic muteness follow.

Because the black child is burdened by the cultural and domestic conspiracy of silence in matters regarding the sexual violation of juveniles, it was to be decades before Angelou could disclose in writing the pain she experienced in this episode. Nevertheless, her honest portrayal of the rape (her sensitivity to the victim at a time when rape victims were generally believed to have seduced their attackers), and her political decision to expose how black males, in the cruelest game of power, violate black females as if they were mere ciphers, making even heavier the crosses they bear, emphasise her courage and initiative as a writer. Angelou poignantly portrays the victim's psychological landscape: first, her need for parental love and intimacy, and later, her confusion, guilt and fear. Even more importantly, Angelou's testimony challenges the practice of suppressing gender in the name of broader racial concerns, as was the case in both the Civil Rights and the Black Power Movements.

Articulating the significance of the rape scene in the book, Angelou says in an interview with George Goodman[9]:

> The real problem in America is between black men and white men. Both see themselves as warriors. Black men talk about change when what they really mean is exchange. They want to take over the positions of power white men have. . . . Now I am going to do what I can to help clear the air in black America because, as I see it, that's what needs to be done. I'm going to write in *Caged Bird* about all those black men with their fists balled up who talk about nation-buildin' time and then go home to rape their nieces and step-daughters and all the little teenage girls who don't know beans about life. I'm going to tell it because rape and incest are rife in the black community.

In the United States race and sex have always been overlapping discourses, a fact that has its origins in slavery.[7] Angelou asserts that the profound impact of rape is best understood in the context of rape as a crime against the person and not the hymen. She correctly depicts rape as a political act by which men attempt to assert their domination over women.

Such effective use of autobiography in consciousness-raising broke what, in retrospect, seems a remarkable silence about a pervasive aspect of the young female experience. It also effectively led to subsequent strategies for change, ranging from feminist self-help methods of rape crisis centres to reform of the criminal justice and medical care systems.[8]

Angelou's analytical grasp of the position of the black woman, based on her childhood trauma, has made her an important spokesperson for second-wave feminism. More importantly, she has spearheaded the rebellion of African-American women against male oppressors by pointing to the complex causes rather than to the camouflage of oppression. She asserts that:

> The Black female is assaulted in her tender years by all those common forces of nature at the same time that she is caught in the tripartite crossfire of masculine prejudice, white illogical hate and black lack of power. The fact that the adult American Negro female emerges a formidable character is often met with amazement, distaste and even belligerence. It is seldom accepted as an inevitable outcome of the struggle won by survivors and deserves respect if not enthusiastic acceptance. (*Caged Bird* 272)

These major setbacks in the young Maya's life are counterbalanced by her scholastic aptitude, encouragement by her teachers, drama and dance classes, culminating in a role in the musical "Porgy and Bess" as a singular achievement in Maya's career in theatre. Reading provides the first step out of the pit of despair. Back in Stamps after the rape, Maya is helped by Momma's friend, Mrs. Flowers, to regain her speech through reciting the poetry she loves so much. Later, in San Francisco, her class teacher, Miss Kirwin, stimulates her intellectually by challenging her to learn about current affairs; while her extra-curricular dance and drama classes teach Maya to be less self-conscious. Repeatedly tossed between city and rural life, Maya learns to identify with both localities. She takes shelter in the "soft breath of anonymity" (*Caged Bird* 212) that shrouds and cushions her bashful self in San Francisco's "air of collective displacement, the impermanence of life in wartime" (211) as surely as she rebuilds her cocoon in the social devastation and barren nothingness of Stamps. Thus Maya creatively reconstitutes the physical landscape as the contestatory site of a decentred subject-in-progress whose homecoming entails painful border-crossings.

Particular incidents that Angelou stresses as triumphs in her adolescence are her adventure in Mexico, her stay in the junkyard, and her successful struggle for employment in the railways. The trip to Mexico involves Maya's manoeuver of her drunken father's car down a treacherous mountain at night. The thrill that she feels after this daring success awakens her potential to control her own destiny.

The second incident results in the acquisition of even greater confidence for she manages to survive a month in a junkyard after being stabbed by her father's girlfriend.[9] Here, the unquestioning acceptance by her displaced peers enables her to find acceptance as an equal in a peaceful, multi-racial community, an experience that also marks the beginnings of racial tolerance in Maya's life. Moreover, the lack of criticism strengthens her ego and makes Maya realize her potential to survive, even without adult support.

The third empowering incident is Maya's relentless determination to challenge the San Francisco Rail company to employ her as its first black streetcar 'conductorette,' which demonstrates the strength of her grow- ing self-esteem. Having taken a semester off from school to work after her sixteen-year-old brother leaves home, Maya finally gets the job she wants and enjoys, at a time when many older black women still endured the drudgery of either domestic and janitorial work or low-level clerkship. This last episode has the benefit of improving Maya's relations with her mother (Vivian is impressed by her daughter's efforts to challenge racism independently); and Suzette Henke pertinently asks: "If discrimination can be overcome by the patient self-assertion of a lone, determined teenager, what might racial soli- darity and communal black struggle for empowerment not achieve?" (213).

Although still young, Maya thus demonstrates the potential for agency precisely because, ironically, she is and always has been so enmeshed in the everyday struggles of black people. Her ability to become the first black 'con- ductorette,' therefore, affirms resources for resistance and hope instead of al- ways showing blacks as victims of oppression in a manner that reproduces the punitive power it critiques. In time, Maya's work success as employee, performer, and writer leads her into the political arena and work with Dr. Martin Luther King in the Civil Rights Movement.

While the foregoing discussion demonstrates Maya's growing self-reliance, it also points to a dramatic contrast between her lack of parental support and Sindiwe's secure family life. Born (in 1943) into a loving peas- ant family, in which she is wanted and cherished, Sindiwe's early confidence is bolstered by an intact extended family as the proximity and cooperation of her maternal and paternal homesteads[10] counterbalance the disruption caused by her father's enforced absence, an unpleasant characteristic of life in South Africa.[11] In fact, since he is the sole breadwinner, his authority as a father figure and provider remains unchallenged. Consequently, despite his absence, she appreciates his overbearing strength, his seriousness, his sense of respon- sibility and his wisdom.

By further contrast, the spiritual force of Christianity in America is lacking in South Africa. Going to church on Sunday is seen as a sorry event unnecessarily disrupting Sindiwe's otherwise perfectly gleeful week. Moreover, in the secure, pastoral setting of her early childhood, evidence of white intrusion is minimal. So again in contrast to Maya's early encounter of a culturally mixed if differentiated society, the cultural practices of the white village store owner, as much as those of the rare tourists who drive through the village, seem so alien in Sindiwe's juvenile mind as to border on the ludicrous. Using the innocent voice of a child to undermine the conventional viewpoint whereby the 'natives' are often presented as spectacle, Magona convincingly reproduces the children's reaction to their first encounter with the tourists who buy their crude crafts as a meeting of equals in commerce. " 'Shwen shwehn-shwehn shwehn,' we heard them say. 'Shwen, Shwen-shwen,' we replied. We addressed them in the gibberish they spoke" (*Children's Children* 12). In this 'We—Them' situation, both parties are secure in their actions. Thus the blissful ignorance of understanding neither the language of the whites[12] nor the monetary value of the coins they receive in exchange for the proffered wares preserves the native children's positive identity or wholesome sense of self. Capturing the psychological protection she enjoyed from having her own distinct culture and language, Magona recalls:

> That whatever they said was nothing I understood simplified our transaction for me. By taking away the need for comprehension, I was left unhindered and unhampered by having to strive for coherence. . . . The logic of a child facilitated what now, as an adult, I find excruciatingly difficult: communication. (11–12)

Sindiwe thus enjoys an innocent childhood, insisting on the strength of her absentee father, and remaining fully aware of the potentially alienating effects of Christianity.[13] Paradoxically, whereas separate development in South Africa enables Sindiwe to see herself as equal to the whites with whom she interacts, democracy in the USA, with its close contact with whites, poses an ever-present hegemonic threat for Maya: "[whites] were to be dreaded, and in that dread was included the hostility of the powerless against the powerful, the poor against the rich, the worker against the worked for and the ragged against the well dressed" (*Caged Bird* 25).

So, sheltered as she is from early awareness of so-called white supremacy, Sindiwe's innocence (developed during her stay in the village) even survives the relocation to the impoverished Blaauveli to which she moves at the age of five with her ailing mother and two siblings. Capturing her incurable optimism at this stage, Sindiwe recalls:

> Despite the glaring gap between the expectations I had harboured
> and the far from swanky reality that was my new life, the
> bubble didn't burst. The belief that our situation had improved
> tremendously persisted despite very strong evidence to the contrary.
> Mere proximity to the splendour of the city mesmerized me with
> promise of attainability. (*Children's Children* 21)

The security of living in a loving, stable nuclear family comforts Sindiwe and
protects her from the negative effects of the squalor, lack of basic facilities
and the general hardship which blacks face in the slums of a city as beautiful
as Cape Town.[14] As a result, even though events such as her younger sister's
death from malnutrition or the destruction of all her family's possessions in
the highly flammable shacks could have given her some indication of her
racial and economic powerlessness, Sindiwe does not deem such occurrences
extraordinary. Commenting on Sindiwe's insistence on having enjoyed a
happy childhood, Alexandra Pentolfe-Aegerter (186–187) notes that

> childhood bliss is premised upon childhood oblivion to the
> construction of racial and gendered identity. . . . The child
> symbolises for Magona, all that the African adult could be if free
> of the fetters of racism, sexism, and class and cultural oppression.
> . . . Despite poverty in the townships, Magona manifests an
> irrepressible 'will to be' in all her activities and perspectives as a
> child; in her very actions lies resistance to circumstances that, were
> she aware of their limitations, might otherwise inhibit agency.

While the family's stability and the communal values of sharing and reci-
procity prolong Sindiwe's psychological innocence—in marked contrast to
Maya's—as she enters adolescence she is gradually forced to acknowledge
her position as an oppressed subject.

However unsettling this may be, the majority status which the blacks
enjoyed (and still enjoy), together with the therapeutic energy released by
holding onto indigenous cultural practices, prevent them from falling apart
as a group. Consequently Sindiwe, unlike Maya, benefits greatly from the
group's resilience, but her decision-making powers are restricted until her
eighteenth year, and it is her parents who determine the nature of her sense of
self. Thus, as already argued, Maya's motives are driven by her own decisions,
whereas Sindiwe's parental protection is so inhibiting that she does not cope
well under pressure. For instance, in her adolescence, she is terrified of the
newly formed gangs that come with the forced relocation to Gugulethu. So,
while San Francisco frees Maya from her long-standing inhibitions, Gugule-

thu throws Sindiwe back into herself, "into the core that only [she] can enter. Where not even lovers can penetrate. Only dread" (*Children's Children* 95).

Magona draws attention to three significant events that, in contrast to Maya's three empowering life experiences, erode her crumbling self-confidence further. The first of these is having to apply for a pass at 18 (1961), which according to the law all Africans were obliged to carry on their persons at all times on pain of arrest.[15] Entering the legal status of adulthood as a second-class citizen, Sindiwe had to comply with laws in the making of which she had neither a say nor representation. The second distressing event involves the drowning of two schoolmates in a pit toilet, thus further dramatizing the disparity between black and white.[16] The third upheaval in Sindiwe's young life is the white referendum in 1960, which saw the establishment of a South African Republic under the Afrikaner to the exclusion of blacks, who comprised 75 percent of its population.

These three events, though not directly linked, are firmly intertwined and have the reverse effect on her perception of any control over her future when compared to Maya's. They are "strands of the same hideous whole," articulating both her voicelessness, "meticulously designed by the powers that be," and "the systematic extinguishing of a breath of a people by rank bigotry and evil incarnate" (*Children's Children* 87).

The political powerlessness of blacks in South Africa has several adverse effects. For example, whereas Maya has easy access to public libraries, books, and the theatre, black people in South Africa did not. This inverse pattern is further reflected in the formal education of the two characters. As a young teenager in California, Maya attends an elite suburban school where she is one of only three black students. Sindiwe, having joined the township exclusively black 'in-crowd,' fails a grade and has to repeat in a secluded multi-racial Catholic boarding school that removes students from meaningful engagement with their traditional environment. Consequently, although Sindiwe completes her schooling and lands a teaching job, she is ill prepared for the responsibilities facing her. The overcrowded classes of poor students, who never have the necessary stationery and books, and the high failure rate, prove the teacher-training course for blacks to be merely a sham. Sindiwe's disillusionment with her chosen career does little to enhance her ego; and the meager salary she earns, determined by her race and gender, does little to compensate for the negative aspects of her life and work.

It is under such circumstances, therefore, that Sindiwe's unplanned premarital pregnancy causes her "world" to go "awry." Living among a people to whom premarital conception is traditionally taboo, Sindiwe's 'fall' is tantamount to death. In terms of gender inequality, it emphasises her powerlessness within the traditional patriarchal system. Her family is disappointed because it can no longer expect as high a bride price for her as it would for a virgin. Older and less educated than she, they marry her off to her lover whose inferior education and menial employment make him an unsuitable husband.[17] Sindiwe's parents' reaction to her pregnancy reveals them as equally powerless over the political[18] and missionary[19] manipulations of existing ethnic practices. Together with Sindiwe, they are thus trapped between modernisation and tradition. Even though she underwent the traditional rites of passage from girlhood to womanhood, when the family gathered to celebrate her first menstrual period, Sindiwe had not been alerted to the connection between menstruation, sexual activity, and pregnancy.

Maya had also become pregnant while still a teenager. Without the benefit of any sex education, she fears her growing vulva means she is a lesbian. The stigma of lesbians drives the sixteen-year-old Maya to unwise decisions: she takes matters into her own hands in an attempt to clarify her sexual orientation. Dissatisfied with her mother's assurances, she seduces a stranger, exploring her sexuality in a manner that underscores the ignorance in which Western-bred girls, whether black or white, are kept regarding their bodies. This, in a sense, is a form of psychological clitoridectomy. On a more subconscious level, Maya's sexual curiosity results from the force of her awakening sexual appetite as much as it reflects the long-term effects of being sexually abused as a child.[20] As a result, she picks a young man she does not know in order to avoid enjoying her 'first' sexual experience, possibly because she associates sex with the pain of rape. Maya's unplanned pregnancy is a clear reflection of the negative effects of her society's insistence on heterosexuality.

Maya's ability to carry her 'immaculate' pregnancy almost to its full term, without any help, is perhaps the ultimate measure of her independence.[21] She has learnt not only to make her own decisions, but also how to bear them and their consequences once they are made. Vivian's support, her provision of neither overt nor subtle condemnation, and her determination to nurture her grandson attest to strong kinship bonds among black families that continue to rebuild the structures that were systematically broken down since the days of slavery. After enduring centuries of illegitimate children due to masters and slave drivers raping the slave women to breed more slaves, black Americans have traditionally been more compassionate in matters of sexual fallibility than either their puritanical white brethren or their African brothers and sisters.[22] Since the extent of support or rejection by family members and relatives is a crucial factor in the functioning and self-esteem of young unwed mothers, it is easy to see how Vivian's support helps Maya cope with her metamorphosis from child to satisfied mother. By contrast, Sindiwe's family's rejection reduces her confidence in her newly acquired status of mother.

As a result, she sees herself as a failure: [23]

A young wife. An expectant mother. No longer employed. I was a housewife. . . . Nothing more. Nothing less. . . . In my clear eyes,

I had fallen. Fallen far short of what I had dreamt of becoming. But, I could see no way out of the quagmire in which, even as I watched myself wallow, I sank deeper and ever deeper, with each passing day. (*Children's Children* 110)

Thus where Maya, enabled by her access to better educational facilities and the emergence of the Civil Rights movement, challenges adverse situations and rises above them, Sindiwe is drawn into the vortex of a socio-political legal system designed to disempower blacks intellectually. Nonetheless, by writing *To My Children's Children*, Magona has not only drawn attention to the plight of black women under apartheid, but has also underscored how ethnic culture today fails to prepare women for more independent roles in the community. How a woman gains strength by rejecting traditional roles becomes the thesis of the remainder of Magona's works; and in the present pandemic of violence and rape, with the added virulence of HIV/AIDS, Sindiwe Magona has opened the way for women of the calibre of a Maya Angelou to protest against their continued victimisation and to claim their right to integrity through self-determination.

Notes

1. The quotation is taken from Isabel Hofmeyr's study, *The Oral Historical Narrative in a South African Chiefdom* (1993).

2. This is in line with Angelou's reference to "the Maya character," whom she envisioned as her "invented self" and as a "symbolic character for every black girl growing up in America" (see Kay).

3. In the times of slavery, religion served as a stimulant for the many rebellions that took place. Escaping to Canada was often seen as a journey towards Canaan, comparable to that of the Biblical Israelites escaping from Egypt. Religion was also a major source of strength during the Civil Rights Movement of the 1950s and 60s, with Dr. Martin Luther King, like Harriet Tubman generations before, symbolising Moses' guidance towards the Promised Land.

4. In order to cope psychologically with their abandonment, the two convince themselves that their parents have died. Otherwise how could they possibly be alive, eating, laughing, and enjoying themselves somewhere else without their children?

5. In her study of the conditions that produce either artists or tyrants, Alice Miller asserts that "the absence or presence of a helping witness in childhood determines whether a mistreated child will become a despot who turns his repressed feelings of helplessness against others or an artist who can tell about his or her suffering" (60).

6. Lynn Bloom (294) also observes that instead of blaming her mother for not being the ideal, nurturing, maternal figure, Maya blames her own imagined deficiencies for the detachment.

7. Dating back to slavery when white men maintained their political and economic power by raping black women as a right and a rite, black men felt emasculated as they could neither protect nor control their own women. Rape was,

therefore, a form of symbolic castration. Consequently, the black man defined his attempt to control (and abuse) black women as reclaiming his lost manhood. For further analysis of this issue, see Hooks (57–64).

8. Angelou registers the insensitivity of the health care staff by showing how instead of sympathising with her, the nurses tell her that she no longer has anything to fear: the worst is over for her. Similarly, Angelou portrays the rape victim's unenviable position in the courtroom in which Mr. Freeman's lawyer ridicules her for not knowing what the rapist was wearing when he raped her.

9. After her father's insecure live-in girlfriend stabs her in the abdomen with a knife during a fight, Maya runs away to a junkyard where she stays until the wound heals. Maya fears Vivian will retaliate if she finds out that her daughter has been wounded.

10. As a toddler, Sindiwe, her mother, older brother and younger sister lived with their extended family—her maternal grandparents, whose homestead she also considers her home.

11. He, like many men who leave the villages in search of employment in the mines, factories, and farms of South Africa, travels to far-away Cape Town where he works a twelve-hour shift as a petrol attendant and yet earns a pittance.

12. The white tourists could have been speaking English or Afrikaans (a South African combination of Dutch, French, and German used by whites of Dutch descent).

13. Although the frightening religious imagery (warnings of death and damnation) employed to convert the 'heathens' had a permanent adverse imprint of Magona's psyche (even now she finds she still cannot relax on Sundays), for many women Christianity later provided valuable support, as women often played important roles in the liturgy.

14. Africanist womanists such as Obioma Nnaemeka challenge the dichotomy between rural and urban. The majority of contemporary urban Africans lack the basic amenities that are taken to characterise urban living (e.g. water-borne sewerage, electricity, and telecommunication services—conditions which are exacerbated by the massive rural exodus with the attendant rapid urban population growth—while they are also denied the serenity (environmental, at least) that marks rural life. Urbanites are, therefore, victims of rural living in a deteriorating urban setting. See Nnaemeka (10).

15. The pass law system was designed to control the availability of the 'native' labour pool. This meant that 'surplus natives' were trespassing in white areas unless they had a valid pass confirming their right to work or reside in that vicinity. Not unnaturally, the system created a feeling of perpetual insecurity in the black community, especially as the law was vigorously enforced.

16. At that time the government subsidised education by providing R480 for a white child and R28 for an African child (*Children's Children* 99). Only white schools had water-borne sewerage systems.

17. Although it is possible that she marries Luthando because she is emotionally attracted to him, Sindiwe' s sense of shame is so strongly expressed (at one point she runs away from home for two weeks) that any positive feelings she had about marrying him are overshadowed.

18. The introduction of contraception in the sixties came shrouded in controversy. The government was enticing Europeans to migrate to South Africa to increase the numbers of the white minority, while blacks were urged to have

fewer children. White families received bonuses for having more than four children (*Children's Children* 64), in addition to being generally protected by the welfare benefits for which only whites qualified.

19. Despite opposing the apartheid government by insisting on the rights of black children to be formally educated, missionaries did the youth a disservice by erasing traditional sex education from the agenda of preparing youth for adult responsibilities. Previously adolescents, often monitored by older youths, were taught sex play (e.g. inserting the penis between the thighs and ejaculating outside the vagina) that satisfied their urges with no risk of unwanted pregnancy and unplanned parenthood.

20. In an interview with George Goodman, Jr.[9], Angelou also admitted that her confusion over her sexual identity was prompted by being sexually assaulted as a child.

21. Fearing that Vivian would restrain her from attending school, she manages to hide the pregnancy from her mother until the ninth month.

22. Suzette A. Henke (214). For statistics showing more support for unwed mothers among black than among white families (who often opted for adoption or abortion), see Hill (24).

23. Since young women were expected to get married and therefore benefit the husband's family, Sindiwe's parents had run counter to tradition by educating daughter when others saw such an investment as a waste of hard-earned money. By qualifying as a teacher, Sindiwe became the first in her family to have a professional certificate.

WORKS CITED

Angelou, Maya. *I Know Why the Caged Bird Sings*. 1969. New York: Bantam Books, 1993.

Bloom, Lynn. "Heritages: Dimensions of Mother-Daughter Relationships in Women's Autobiographies." *The Lost Tradition: Mothers and Daughters in Literature*. Ed. Cathy N. Davidson and E. M. Broner. New York: Ungar, 1980. 291–303.

Elliot, Jeffrey, ed. *Conversations with Maya Angelou*. Jackson: University Press of Mississippi, 1989.

Goodman, George. 1972. "Interview with George Goodman, Jr." *Conversations with Maya Angelou*. Ed. Jeffrey Elliot. Conversations with Maya Angelou. Jackson: University Press of Mississippi, 1989.

Henke, Suzette A. "Women's Life Writing and the Minority Voice: Maya Angelou, Maxine Hong Kingston, and Alice Walker." *Traditions, Voices, and Dreams: The American Novel since the 1960s*. Ed. Melvin J. Friedman. Newark, N.J.: Delaware University Press, 1995. 210–233.

Hill, Robert B. *The Strength of Black Families*. New York: Emerson Hall, 1971.

Hill-Lubin, Mildred A. "The Grandmother in African and African-American Literature: A Survivor of the African Extended Family." *Ngambika: Studies of Women in African Literature*. Ed. Carole Boyce Davies and Anne Adams Graves. Trenton, N.J.: Africa World Press, 1986. 257–270.

Hofmeyr, Isabel. *The Oral Historical Narrative in a South African Chiefdom*. Portsmouth: Heinemann; Johannesburg: Witwatersrand University Press; London: James Currey, 1993.

hooks, bell. "Reflections of Race and Sex." *Yearnings: Race, Gender and Cultural Politics*. Boston: South End Press, 1990.

Kay, Jackie. "'The Maya Character': Interview with Jackie Kay." *Conversations with Maya Angelou*. Ed. Jeffrey Elliot. Jackson: University Press of Mississippi, 1989. 194–200.

Magona, Sindiwe. *To My Children's Children*. Cape Town: David Philip, 1990.

Miller, Alice. *The Untouched Key*. New York: Doubleday, 1990.

Nnaemeka, Obioma. *Sisterhood: Feminists and Power from African to the Diaspora*. Trenton, N.J.: Africa World Press, 1989.

Pentolfe-Aegerter, Alexandra. "'You Have Met the Woman: You Have Struck the Rock': Southern African Women's Writing as Resistance." Thesis University of Washington, 1992.

LUCINDA MOORE

A Conversation with Maya Angelou at 75

Turning 75 this month, Maya Angelou has led many lives. She is best known as a writer, for her numerous books of poetry and her six poignant memoirs, including the masterful 1969 *I Know Why the Caged Bird Sings*. In February, she won a Grammy for the recorded reading of her most recent memoir, *A Song Flung Up to Heaven*. Her works have earned her more than 30 honorary degrees as well as nominations for a National Book Award and a Pulitzer Prize. She wrote "On the Pulse of Morning" for the 1993 swearing-in of President Bill Clinton, becoming only the second poet in U. S. history—Robert Frost was the first, for John F. Kennedy—invited to compose an inaugural poem.

Less well known are Angelou's other lives: as a singer; as a composer; as a dancer in *Porgy and Bess;* as an actor in the Obie-winning play *The Blacks* and in films such as *Calypso Heat Wave* and *How to Make an American Quilt;* as a civil rights worker with Martin Luther King, Jr.; as a journalist in Egypt and Ghana; as a writer for television and Hollywood; as director of the 1998 film *Down in the Delta.* Angelou is the Reynolds Professor of American Studies at North Carolina's Wake Forest University in Winston-Salem. She is constantly on the lecture circuit and a regular guest on talk shows; she recently created a line of greeting cards for Hallmark. And there is little sign of her slowing down.

Smithsonian, Volume 34, Number 1 (April 2003): p. 96. © 2003 Smithsonian Institution.

But when we met recently in her art-filled home in Winston-Salem, it was her family, not her varied career, that she most wanted to discuss. Our conversation often returned to the loved ones who helped her triumph over the tragedies of her childhood and made her believe she could meet whatever challenge life threw in her path.

Her grandmother Annie Henderson was one of the most important, a pious woman who ran a general store in Stamps, Arkansas. Angelou lived most of her childhood with her grandmother, whom she called "Momma." Angelou's sometimes-absentee mother, Vivian Baxter, had a steel will and several careers of her own. She was an inadvertent player in an early, formative trauma in Angelou's life. When Angelou was 8 and briefly living with Baxter in St. Louis, her mother's boyfriend raped Angelou. The man was arrested, convicted and released; soon after, he was found beaten to death. Believing she had caused the killing because she had told of the rape, Angelou refused to speak for several years; only her beloved older brother, Bailey, could coax her to talk. He remained a source of support throughout her life until his death more than a year ago. And there is Angelou's son, Guy Johnson, 57, author of *Echoes of a Distant Summer* and one other novel. He is, she says, her "monument in the world."

MOORE: You've said that society's view of the black woman is such a threat to her well-being that she will die daily unless she determines how she sees herself. How do you see yourself?

ANGELOU: I just received a letter yesterday from the University of Milan. A person is doing a doctoral dissertation on my work. It's called *Sapienza,* which means wisdom. I'm considered wise, and sometimes I see myself as knowing. Most of the time, I see myself as wanting to know. And I see myself as a very interested person. I've never been bored in my life.

MOORE: You have never been bored? How is that possible?

ANGELOU: Oh God, if I were bored, now that would interest me. I'd think, my God, how did that happen and what's going on? I'd be caught up in it. Are you kidding? Bored?

I realized when I was about 20 that I would die. It frightened me so. I mean, I had heard about it, had been told and all that, but that I . . . ? [She points at herself and raises her brows as if in disbelief.] It so terrified me that I double-locked the doors; I made certain that the windows were double-locked—trying to keep death out—and finally I admitted that there was nothing I could do about it. Once I really came to that conclusion, I started enjoying life, and I enjoy it very much.

Another occurrence took place at about the same time—maybe about a year later—and the two occurrences liberated me forever.

I had two jobs. I was raising my son. We had a tiny little place to live. My mother had a 14-room house and someone to look after things. She owned a hotel, lots of diamonds. I wouldn't accept anything from her. But once a month she'd cook for me. And I would go to her house and she'd be dressed beautifully.

One day after we'd had lunch, she had to go somewhere. She put on silver-fox furs—this was when the head of one fox would seem to bite into the head of the other—and she would wear them with the tails in front; she would turn it around with the furs arching back. We were halfway down the hill and she said, "Baby"—and she was small; she was 5-feet-4 ½ and I'm 6 foot—"You know something? I think you're the greatest woman I've ever met." We stopped. I looked down at this pretty little woman made up so perfectly, diamonds in her ears. She said, "Mary McLeod Bethune, Eleanor Roosevelt, my mother and you—you are the greatest." It still brings me to te—. [Her eyes tear up.]

We walked down to the bottom of the hill. She crossed the street to the right to get into her car. I continued across the street and waited for the streetcar. And I got onto the streetcar and I walked to the back. I shall never forget it. I remember the wooden planks of the streetcar. The way the light came through the window. And I thought, suppose she's right? She's very intelligent, and she's too mean to lie. Suppose I really am somebody?

Those two incidents liberated me to think large thoughts, whether I could comprehend them or not [she laughs], but to think. . . .

MOORE: One of your large thoughts must have been about planning to have a diverse life and career. How do you move so easily from one thing to another?

ANGELOU: I have a theory that nobody understands talent any more than we understand electricity. So I think we've done a real disservice to young people by telling them, "Oh, you be careful. You'll be a jack-of-all-trades and a master of none." It's the stupidest thing I've ever heard. I think you can be a jack-of-all-trades and a mistress-of-all-trades. If you study it, and you put reasonable intelligence and reasonable energy, reasonable electricity to it, you can do that. You may not become Max Roach on the drums. But you can learn the drums. I've long felt that way about things. If I'm asked, "Can you do this?" I think, if I don't do it, it'll be ten years before another black woman is asked to do it. And I say, yes, yes, when do you want it?

My mom, you know, was a seaman. At one point, I was in Los Angeles. I called her in San Francisco and said, I want to see you, I'm going to New York and I don't know when I'll be back, so let's meet mid-state. She said, "Oh, baby, I wanted to see you, too, because I'm going to sea." I said, going to see what? She said, "I'm going to become a seaman." I said, Mother, really, come on. She said, "No, they told me they wouldn't let women in their union. I told them, 'You wanna bet?' I put my foot in that door up to my hip so women of every color will get in that union, get aboard a ship and go to sea." She retired in 1980, and Asian, white and black women gave a party for her. They called her the mother of the sea.

So, yes, we cripple our children, we cripple each other with those designations that if you're a brick mason you shouldn't love the ballet. Who made that rule? You ever see a person lay bricks? [She moves her hands in a precise bricklaying manner.] Because of the eye and the hands, of course he or she would like to see ballet. It is that precise, that established, that organized, that sort of development from the bottom to the top.

MOORE: Do you resent the fact that your mother wasn't there for much of your childhood?

ANGELOU: Oh, yes. Yes. I was an abandoned child as far as I was concerned, and Bailey also. We didn't hear from her—we heard maybe twice in seven years or something. And then I realized that she was funny and loving and that there are certainly two different kinds of parents. There is the person who can be a great parent of small children. They dress the children in these sweet little things with bows in their hair and beads on their shoestrings and nice, lovely little socks. But when those same children get to be 14 or 15, the parents don't know what to say to them as they grow breasts and testosterone hits the boy.

Well, my mom was a terrible parent of young children. And thank God—I thank God every time I think of it—I was sent to my paternal grandmother. Ah, but my mother was a great parent of a young adult. When she found out I was pregnant, she said, "All right. Run me a bath, please." Well, in my family, that's really a very nice thing for somebody to ask you to do. Maybe two or three times in my life she had asked me to run her a bath. So I ran her a bath and then she invited me in the bathroom. My mother sat down in the bathtub. She asked me, "Do you love the boy?" I said no. "Does he love you?" I said no. "Well, there's no point in ruining three lives. We're going to have us a baby."

And she delivered Guy—because she was a nurse also. She took me to the hospital. It was during one of the Jewish holidays, and my doctor wasn't there. My mother went in, told the nurses who she was, she washed up, they took me into the delivery room. She got up on the table on her knees with me and put her shoulder against my knee and took my hand, and every time a pain would come she'd tell a joke. I would laugh and laugh [she laughs uproariously] and bear down. And she said, "Here he comes, here he comes." And she put her hand on him first, my son.

So throughout her life she liberated me. Liberated me constantly. Respected me, respected what I tried to do, believed in me. I'd go out in San Francisco—I'd be visiting her, I was living in Los Angeles—and stay really late at some after-hours joint. Mother knew all of them and knew all the bartenders. And I'd be having a drink and laughing, and the bartender would say on the phone, "Yeah, Mama, yeah she's here." She'd say to me: "Baby, it's your mother. Come home. Let the streets know you have somewhere to go."

MOORE: It seems your mother and Bailey always came to your rescue. Were they more vigilant, do you think, because you didn't speak for so long?

ANGELOU: All those years ago I'd been a mute, and my mother and my brother knew that in times of strife and extreme stress, I was likely to retreat to mutism. Mutism is so addictive. And I don't think its powers ever go away. It's as if it's just behind my view, just behind my right shoulder or my left shoulder. If I move quickly, it moves, so I can't see it. But it's always there saying, "You can always come back to me. You have nothing to do—just stop talking." So, when I've been in stress, my mother or my brother, or both sometimes, would come wherever I was, New York, California, anywhere, and say, "Hello, hello, talk to me. Come on, let's go. We'll have a game of Scrabble or pinochle and let's talk. Tell me a story." Because they were astute enough to recognize the power of mutism, I finally was astute enough to recognize the power of their love.

MOORE: What went through your mind during the years you were mute?

ANGELOU: Oh, yes, I memorized poetry. I would test myself, memorizing a conversation that went by when I wasn't in it. I memorized 60 Shakespearean sonnets. And some of the things I memorized, I'd never heard them spoken, so I memorized them according to the cadence that I heard in my head. I loved Edgar Allan Poe and I memorized everything I could find. And I loved Paul Laurence Dunbar—still do—so I would memorize 75 poems. It was like putting a CD on. If I wanted to, I'd just run through my memory and think, that's one I want to hear.

So I believe that my brain reconstructed itself during those years. I believe that the areas in the brain which provide and promote physical speech had nothing to do. I believe that the synapses of the brain, instead of just going from A to B, since B wasn't receptive, the synapses went from A to R. You see what I mean? And so, I've been able to develop a memory quite unusual, which has allowed me to learn languages, really quite a few. I seem to be able to direct the brain; I can say, do that. I say, remember this, remember that. And it's caught! [She snaps her fingers as if to emphasize "caught."]

MOORE: You lived with your grandmother during your silent years. How did she respond?

ANGELOU: She said, "Sister, Momma don't care what these people say, that you must be an idiot, a moron, 'cause you can't talk. Momma don't care. Momma know that when you and the good Lord get ready, you gon' be a teacher."

MOORE: If your mother liberated you to think big, what gifts did your grandmother give you?

ANGELOU: She gave me so many gifts. Confidence that I was loved. She taught me not to lie to myself or anyone else and not to boast. She taught me to admit that, to me, the emperor has no clothes. He may be dressed in the finery of the ages to everybody else, but if I don't see it, to admit that I don't see it. Because of her, I think, I have remained a very simple woman. What you see is all there is. I have no subterfuge. And she taught me not to complain.

My grandmother had one thing that she would do for me about twice a year. Shall I tell you? [She laughs loudly.] Momma would see a whiner, a complainer come down the hill. And she would call me in. She'd say, "Sister, Sister, come out here." I'd go and look up the hill and a complainer was trudging. And the man or woman would come into the store, and my grandmother would ask, "How you feel today?"

"Ah, Sister Henderson, I tell you I just hate the winter. It makes my face crack and my shins burn."

And Momma'd just say, "Uh-huh," and then look at me. And as soon as the person would leave, my grandmother would say, "Sister, come here." I'd stand right in front of her. She'd say, "There are people all over the world who went to sleep last night who did not wake again. Their beds have become their cooling boards, their blankets have become their winding sheets. They would give anything for just five minutes of what she was complaining about."

MOORE: Did you write during your childhood?

ANGELOU: Well, I've always written. There's a journal which I kept from about 9 years old. The man who gave it to me lived across the street from the store and kept it when my grandmother's papers were destroyed. I'd written some essays. I loved poetry, still do. But I really, really loved it then. I would write some—of course it was terrible—but I'd always written something down.

MOORE: I read that you wrote the inaugural poem, "On the Pulse of Morning," in a hotel room. Were you on the road when you composed it?

ANGELOU: I keep a hotel room here in Winston when I'm writing. I take a room for about a month. And I try to be in the room by 6 a.m., so I get up, make coffee and keep a thermos and I go out to the hotel. I would have had everything removed from the room, wall hangings and all that stuff. It's just a bed, a table and a chair, *Roget's Thesaurus,* a dictionary, a bottle of sherry, a yellow pad and pens, and I go to work. And I work 'til about twelve or one; one if it's going well, twelve if it isn't. Then I come home and pretend to operate in the familiar, you know?

MOORE: Where does writing rank in your accomplishments?

ANGELOU: I'm happy to be a writer, of prose, poetry, every kind of writing. Every person in the world who isn't a recluse, hermit or mute uses words. I know of no other art form that we always use. So the writer has to take the most used, most familiar objects—nouns, pronouns, verbs, adverbs—ball them together and make them bounce, turn them a certain way and make people get into a romantic mood; and another way, into a bellicose mood. I'm most happy to be a writer.

CLARENCE NERO

A Discursive Trifecta: Community, Education, and Language in I Know Why the Caged Bird Sings

Maya Angelou's writing transcends race, gender, class, and culture. There have been few writers—living or dead—who have commanded the written word with such vigor and definitive purpose. She has lived every noun, verb, adjective, and adverb on her pages, and the body of work has a literary aesthetic of its own that is inextricably linked to the African-American tradition of storytelling. Dr. Angelou's writing is on the level of discursiveness, which the *American Heritage Dictionary* describes as "a verbal expression in speech and writing." In taking a closer look at *I Know Why the Caged Bird Sings* (1970) we find community, education, and language working as a "discursive trifecta" to bring dignity, hope, and pride to a black community "fragmented by Diaspora' (Folks 1).

Caged Bird was the first in a series of autobiographical portraits of the life and history of a phenomenal woman with a strong sense of community and pride. Dr. Angelou's life has been a testimony to the strength and tenacity of the human spirit to rise in the face of adversity. She grew up during an era of much racial tension and oppression. She was dirt poor and shuffled between the homes of her birth mother in California and grandmother in Stamps, Arkansas. She was raped and left mute for years, but from all the tragedies and despair, Angelou survived this harsh reality through the "triumphant spirit of her community's endurance" (Eller 3). The community's

The Langston Hughes Review, Volume 19 (Spring 2005): pp. 61–65. © 2005 Langston Hughes Review.

117

involvement in establishing the young Marguerite's (Maya Angelou's) identity is noteworthy because it contributes to a discursive trifecta that shows the importance of communal affirmation in maintaining the African American community.

George Gutman notes in his book, *The Black Family in Slavery and Freedom, 1750–1925* (1976), that community has always been necessary for the survival of black culture formed out of slavery:

> Developing Afro-American behavior patterns were reinforced by the development of Afro-American slave institutions that took their shape within the parameters of the masters' monopoly of power, but separate from the masters' institutions, and the emergence of such communities defined the moment when Africans can be described as Afro-Americans. (4)

The behavior pattern that "was reinforced by the slaves" is the emergence of a black folk tradition—expressed through songs and religious hymns—and separate from that of the dominant culture (4). In fact, these songs of inspiration provided a means for blacks to resolve their "conflict of white perceptions and actions" (Eller 3).

Consequently, in looking at Angelou's *Caged Bird* there exists a thematic unity of subtle racial resistance along with the establishment of pride and identity mainly conveyed through the medium of songs and music (Walker 3). In chapter 18, with poignant detail Angelou recalls words that moved her at a church revival: "Bye and Bye, when the morning come/when all the saints of God's are gathering home/we will tell the story of how we overcome and we'll understand it better bye and bye" (129). What made this revival enriching and memorable for Angelou was its bringing together a community of blacks from all religious backgrounds. Angelou writes in *Caged Bird:*

> Everyone attended the revival meetings. Members of the hoity-toity Mount Zion Baptist Church mingled with the intellectual members of The African Methodist Episcopal and African Methodist Episcopal Zion, and the plain working people of the Christian Methodist Episcopal. These gatherings provided the one time in the year when all of those good village people associated with the followers of the Church of God in Christ. (123–124)

Many other relevant examples illustrate the importance of community in developing Marguerite's identity; for instance, Angelou's Grandmother Henderson ran a small country store in Stamps where she was the backbone of the community. When hard times befell anyone, they turned to her for assistance. Grandmother Henderson was indeed strong and supportive. Angelou highlights her firm religious beliefs as significant in dealing with overt oppression and racial hostility. In fact, Chapter 5 illuminates religious hymns as a discursive device in fighting racism "with a dignified course of silent endurance" (McPherson 33).

The scene with the "powhitetrash" girls (32), who corner Grandmother Henderson in her own front yard throwing insults and racial slander, was included to show the power of faith, which has always been at the heart and fabric of the black community. While the "powhitetrash" girls taunt and tease, Grandmother Henderson responds by humming a quiet hymn: "Glory, glory, hallelujah, when I lay my burden down" (33). Angelou notes that there was a contest between the girls and her grandmother, a contest that Grandmother Henderson wins (33). As a black woman, Grandmother Henderson must "perform" respect towards the children who should be showing her genuine respect, but she uses the vehicle of song as a mechanism to triumph over her restrictions and limitations (McMurry 3). Elizabeth Fox-Genovese notes in her essay, "Myth and History: Discourse of Origins in Zora Neale Hurston and Maya Angelou," that there has always been this singing tradition in the black community: "Black communities developed their own vibrant life, black women raised up black girls in the way that they should go/Singing in the face of danger, singing to thwart the stings of insolence, singing to celebrate their Lord, singing to testify to a better future, and singing with the life blood of their people" (222). Even though Grandmother Henderson could not overtly display her dislike towards the "powhitetrash" girls, she taught Angelou how to stand in the midst of adversity and how to calm the spirit in the face of ignorance. The most significant display of communal affirmation and the power of song as a force comes with the graduation scene in *Caged Bird*, a scene often referenced by scholars in discussions of the "subtle racial resistance" intertwined throughout the novels' themes (Walker 7). Moreover, the graduation scene valorizes education, language, and community as a discursive trifecta in elevating an oppressed and deprived people to a level of worthiness and respect.

Slave masters understood that "knowledge is power," and through communication access to the world is gained. They therefore denied slaves the right to available forms of education. The canon of black literature responded by making education an important symbol affirming the black identity and demonstrating black intelligence and ability to survive within American culture. This symbolism stretches across a broad spectrum of literary aesthetics ranging from poetry to fiction and including African American autobiographies. In *Caged Bird*, Angelou's recollection of her eighth grade graduation bears heavily upon this discussion of education as an important discursive element.

We must remember that this graduation was taking place during a time of much racial tension in America, when Jim Crow laws and the notion of separate but equal were still a reality for African American citizens. Regardless of this fact, however, Angelou recalls how proud she was of her achievement and how important graduation was to the entire community:

> Parents who could not afford it had ordered new shoes and ready-made clothes for themselves from Sears Roebuck or Montgomery Ward. They also engaged the best seamstresses to make the floating graduating dresses and to cut down secondhand pants which would be pressed to a military slickness for the important event. [. . .] oh, it was important, all right. (171)

Unknown to Angelou and the community, the graduation was about to take an unexpected turn when an uninvited guest, Mr. Edward Donleavy, took the podium. A racist politician Donleavy is quickly reminds Marguerite and the other graduates of their limited possibilities despite the achievement of a formal education: "Donleavy had exposed us. We were maids and farmers, handymen, and washerwomen, and anything higher that we aspired to was farcical and presumptuous" (180). This incident was immediately followed by Henry Reed's valedictory address. He leads the students, parents, and visitors in a rendition of James Weldon Johnson's "Lift Ev'ry Voice and Sing," which bonded "the community with a common soul" (Walker 4): "We have come over a way that with tears has been watered/We have come, treading our path through the blood of the slaughtered." This act of employing song to avert racism makes the graduation a scene of communal resistance (Walker 8). Having seen the profound impact that song had in bringing together the black community, Angelou developed a deep respect for literacy and song at an early age: "Oh, Black known and unknown poets, how often have your auctioned pains sustained us? It may be enough, however, to have it said that we survive in exact relationship to the dedication of our poets" (184). Angelou and the graduates were proud of their achievement because they used words and songs as a communal affirmation to produce a positive outcome in the face of prejudice.

This awareness of the power of language and education occurs in an earlier section of the book as well. With Ms. Flowers's chapter, Angelou harnesses a greater respect for literature and the power that words (language) have in transforming a reality of hopeless shame to one of empowerment. It was under Ms. Flowers's guidance that formal education became Angelou's salvation. Ms. Flowers taught Angelou to embrace the spoken and written word and not allow language to be a stumbling block in her development:

Bear in mind that language is man's way of communicating with his fellow man and it is language alone that separates him from the lower animals [. . .]. Words mean more than what is set down on paper. It takes that human voice to infuse them with the shades of deeper meaning. (82)

Ms. Flowers became the catalyst that gave Angelou the courage to transcend her muteness and begin speaking once again, an illustration of language and education as a discursive medium establishing identity and worthiness. Ms. Flowers's speech and their shared reading made Angelou appreciative of literature and proud of her heritage: "I was liked, and what a difference it made. I was respected [. . .] for just being Marguerite Johnson. [. . . S]he made me proud to be Negro, just by being herself" (79, 85). Through poetic verse, education (which was mostly self-taught through reading), and a long-standing appreciation of black history, Angelou freed herself from the cage of her own imperfections, insecurities, and doubts of self-loathing to find authentic inner peace.

Angelou has used that knowledge to craft a banner of hope for all humanity, for the underprivileged, the broken, the educated, the homeless, the rich. Her legacy stretches from urban streets to the continent to Africa. Her history is America's history.

Works Cited

Eller, Edward. "An Overview of *I Know Why The Caged Bird Sings*." *Exploring Novels*. New York: Gale, 1998.

Folks, Jeffrey J. "Communal Responsibility in Ernest J. Gaines's *A Lesson Before Dying*." *Mississippi Quarterly* 52 (1999): 259–272.

Genovese, Elizabeth. "Myth and History: Discourse of Origins in Zora Neale Hurston and Maya Angelou." *Black American Literature Forum* 24.2 (1999): 221–235.

Gutman, Herbert George. *The Black Family in Slavery and Freedom, 1750–1925*. New York: Pantheon Books, 1976.

McMurry, Myra. "Role-Playing as Art in Maya Angelou's *Caged Bird*." *South Atlantic Bulletin* 2 (1976): 106–111.

McPherson, Dolly A. *Order out of Chaos: The Autobiographical Works of Maya Angelou*. New York: Peter Lang, 1990.

Walker, Pierre A. "Racial Protest, Identity, Words, and Form in Maya Angelou's *I Know Why the Caged Bird Sings*." *College Literature* 22.3 (1995): 91–121.

Chronology

1928   Maya Angelou is born Marguerite Johnson on April 1 in St. Louis, Missouri, the daughter of Bailey and Vivian Baxter Johnson.

1931   Her parents divorce; Angelou and her four-year-old brother are sent to live with their maternal grandmother, Annie Henderson, in Stamps, Arkansas.

1936   During a visit to her mother in St. Louis, Angelou is raped by her mother's boyfriend. The man is beaten to death by her uncles and Angelou does not speak for almost five years. She returns to Stamps and discovers literature under the tutelage of an educated neighbor, Mrs. Flowers.

1940   Graduates from the eighth grade at the top of her class. Her mother, now a professional gambler, takes the children to live in San Francisco.

1940–1944   Attends George Washington High School in San Francisco and takes dance and drama lessons at the California Labor School.

1945   While still in high school, becomes the first black woman streetcar conductor in San Francisco; graduates from Mission High School at age 16; one month later, gives birth to a son.

1946	Works as a cook for $75 per week at the Creole Cafe; with $200 she moves to San Diego.
1947	After becoming involved in prostitution as a madam, Angelou returns to Stamps. She upbraids a rude white store clerk; her grandmother, fearing reprisals from the Ku Klux Klan, sends her back to San Francisco.
1948	Joins a nightclub dance act; then works as a restaurant cook; spends several days as a prostitute, until her brother threatens violence if she continues.
1950	Marries Tosh Angelos; they divorce three years later.
1953	Angelou resumes her career as a dancer at the Purple Onion.
1954–1955	Joins a twenty-two-nation tour of *Porgy and Bess,* sponsored by the U.S. Department of State.
1955	Returns to care for her young son, Guy; becomes instructor of Modern Dance at the Rome Opera House and at Hambina Theatre, Tel Aviv.
1957	Appears in a play, *Calypso Heatwave.* Makes a commitment to become a writer and black civil rights activist; moves to Brooklyn and participates in the Harlem Writers' Guild, a group that included John Henrik Clarke, Paule Marshall, James Baldwin, and social activist author John Killens.
1959–1960	Succeeds Bayard Rustin as northern coordinator of Martin Luther King Jr.'s, Southern Christian Leadership Conference.
1960	Appears in the Off-Broadway production of *The Blacks;* produces and performs Off-Broadway in *Cabaret for Freedom,* written with Godfrey Cambridge.
1961–1962	Associate editor of the *Arab Observer,* an English-language newspaper in Cairo, Egypt.
1963–1966	Assistant administrator of the School of Music and Drama at the University of Ghana's Institute of African Studies at Legon-Accra, Ghana. Feature editor of the *African Review;* contributor to the Ghanian Broadcasting Company.
1964	Appears in *Mother Courage* at the University of Ghana.
1966	Appears in *Medea* and *The Least of These* in Hollywood; lecturer at the University of California, Los Angeles.

1970	Writer in residence at the University of Kansas; receives Yale University fellowship; *I Know Why the Caged Bird Sings* is published and nominated for a National Book Award.
1971	A volume of poetry, *Just Give Me a Cool Drink of Water 'Fore I Diiie* is published and nominated for a Pulitzer Prize.
1972	Television narrator, interviewer, and host for African American specials and theater series.
1973	Receives a Tony Award nomination for her Broadway debut in *Look Away*. Marries Paul Du Feu in December; they divorce in 1981.
1974	*Gather Together in My Name* is published; directs the film *All Day Long;* appears in the adapted Sophocles play *Ajax* at the Mark Taper Forum; named distinguished visiting professor at Wake Forest University, Wichita State University, and California State University.
1975	A volume of poetry, *Oh Pray My Wings Are Gonna Fit Me Well,* is published; appointed by President Gerald R. Ford to the American Revolution Bicentennial Council; member of the National Commission on the Observance of International Women's Year; becomes member of the board of trustees of the American Film Institute; appointed Rockefeller Foundation Scholar in Italy; receives honorary degrees from Smith College and Mills College.
1976	*Singin' and Swingin' and Gettin' Merry Like Christmas* is published; directs her play, *And I Still Rise;* named Woman of the Year in Communications; receives honorary degree from Lawrence University.
1977	Appears in the television film *Roots,* and receives a Tony Award nomination for best supporting actress.
1978	*And Still I Rise* is published.
1981	*The Heart of a Woman* is published. Angelou receives a lifetime appointment as Reynolds Professor of American Studies, Wake Forest University.
1983	*Shaker, Why Don't You Sing?,* a volume of poetry, is published. Angelou is named one of the Top 100 Most Influential Women by the *Ladies' Home Journal;* receives the Matrix Award.

1986	*All God's Children Need Travelin' Shoes; Mrs. Flowers: A Moment of Friendship; Poems: Maya Angelou* are published.
1987	*Now Sheba Sings the Song* is published; receives the North Carolina Award in Literature.
1988	Directs Errol John's *Moon on a Rainbow Shawl* in London.
1990	A volume of poetry, *I Shall Not Be Moved*, is published.
1993	The inaugural poem *On the Pulse of Morning; Soul Looks Back in Wonder*, poems and *Wouldn't Take Nothing for My Journey Now* are published. Angelou contributes poetry to the film *Poetic Justice*.
1994	*My Painted House, My Friendly Chicken, and Me* and *Phenomenal Women: Four Poems Celebrating Women* are published.
1995	*A Brave and Startling Truth* is published.
1996	*Kofi and His Magic*, a children's story, is published.
1999	Angelou is presented Lifetime Achievement Award for Literature and is named one of the 100 best writers of the twentieth century by *Writer's Digest*.
2000	A new edition of *Phenomenal Woman: Four Poems Celebrating Women*, edited by Linda Sunshine and with paintings by Paul Gaugin is published, and Angelou is presented the National Medal of Arts.
2002	*A Song Flung up to Heaven*, the final volume of Angelou's biography, is published; she wins a Grammy Award for her recording of it.
2004	*I Know Why the Caged Bird Sings: The Collected Autobiographies of Maya Angelou* is published.
2005	*Amazing Peace* is published.
2006	Angelou's *Amazing Peace* wins Quill Award for poetry.

Contributors

HAROLD BLOOM is Sterling Professor of the Humanities at Yale University. He is the author of 30 books, including *Shelley's Mythmaking* (1959), *The Visionary Company* (1961), *Blake's Apocalypse* (1963), *Yeats* (1970), *A Map of Misreading* (1975), *Kabbalah and Criticism* (1975), *Agon: Toward a Theory of Revisionism* (1982), *The American Religion* (1992), *The Western Canon* (1994), and *Omens of Millennium: The Gnosis of Angels, Dreams, and Resurrection* (1996). *The Anxiety of Influence* (1973) sets forth Professor Bloom's provocative theory of the literary relationships between the great writers and their predecessors. His most recent books include *Shakespeare: The Invention of the Human* (1998), a 1998 National Book Award finalist; *How to Read and Why* (2000); *Genius: A Mosaic of One Hundred Exemplary Creative Minds* (2002); *Hamlet: Poem Unlimited* (2003); *Where Shall Wisdom Be Found?* (2004); and *Jesus and Yahweh: The Names Divine* (2005). In 1999, Professor Bloom received the prestigious American Academy of Arts and Letters Gold Medal for Criticism. He has also received the International Prize of Catalonia, the Alfonso Reyes Prize of Mexico, and the Hans Christian Andersen Bicentennial Prize of Denmark.

LUCINDA H. MACKETHAN is alumni distinguished professor of English at North Carolina State University. Her publications include *The Dream of Arcady: Place and Time in Southern Literature* (1980), with James A. Miller, *Daughters of Time: Creating Woman's Voice in Southern Story* (1990), and *A Guide to Scribbling Women: A Multi-Media Presentation of American Women's Short Stories* (1997).

SHIRLEY J. (S. J.) CORDELL-ROBINSON teaches English and French at James Monroe High School in Fredericksburg, Virginia and serves as president of the Fredericksburg Education Association.

CAROL E. NEUBAUER is assistant professor of English and foreign languages at Bradley University. In addition to her publications on Maya Angelou, she has written articles on Maxine Hong Kingston and Kenyan autobiography.

JOANNE MEGNA-WALLACE is assistant professor of English at Bradford College in Massachusetts. She has written articles on Simone de Beauvoir, and she is a member of the Beauvoir Society executive board.

ELIZABETH FOX-GENOVESE was the Eléonore Raoul professor of the humanities at Emory University. In 1986, she founded the university's Institute for Women's Studies and was its director until 1991. Her several books include *Within the Plantation Household: Black and White Women of the Old South* (1988), *To Be Worthy of God's Favor: Southern Women's Defense and Critique of Slavery* (1993), *Feminism Without Illusions: A Critique of Individualism* (1991), and with her husband Eugene Genovese, *The Mind of the Master Class: History and Faith in the Southern Slaveholders* (2005). In 2003 President George W. Bush awarded her the National Humanities Medal. Fox-Genovese died in 2007.

BONNIE BRAENDLIN is professor of English, emerita, at Florida State University. Over a period of some thirty years, she published many articles, notably on literature and film and topics in modern literature. She wrote *Authority and Transgression in Literature and Film* (1996).

IAN MARSHALL is professor of English and Environmental Studies at Pennsylvania State University, Altoona. He has published many articles, concentrating on topics related to literature and the environment. He wrote *Story Line: Exploring the Literature of the Appalachian Trail* (1998) and *Peak Experiences: Walking Meditations on Literature, Nature, and Need* (2003).

MARCIA ANN GILLESPIE is professor of diversity in residence for the Johnetta B. Cole Global Diversity and Inclusion Institute at Bennett College. She wrote the authorized biography, *Maya Angelou: A Glorious Celebration* (2008). She was editor in chief of *Essence* magazine (1971–1980) and *Ms.* (1993–2001). Her many awards include the Matrix Award from New York Women in Communication, and the Mary MacLeod Bethune Award from the National Council of Negro Women.

ONITA ESTES-HICKS is chair of the department of English at State University of New York, Old Westbury. In addition to African American autobiography, she has written on Jean Toomer.

CASSIE PREMO-STEELE is the author of five books: *Moon Days*, (1999); *We Heal From Memory*, (2000); *Ruin*, (2004); *My Peace*, (2008); and *Easyhard*, (2009). She has also published numerous works on the themes of mothering, nature, and healing through creativity. Premo-Steele currently teaches courses in Ecopoetry and Advanced Writing at the University of South Carolina's Green Learning Center.

DANA CHAMBLEE-CARPENTER is professor of English at Libscomb University. In addition to articles on Maya Angelou and Eudora Welty, she has written award-winning short fiction.

SIPHOKAZI KOYANA is a research fellow in English at the University of Pretoria and has done research on black South African and African American women writers. Her 1999 dissertation at Temple University was "The Heart of a Woman: Black Women's Lives in the United States and South Africa as Portrayed in the Autobiographies of Maya Angelou and Sindiwe Magona."

ROSEMARY GRAY is professor of English and head of research at the University of Pretoria, where she is also the president of the English Academy. She has written extensively on African literature.

LUCINDA MOORE was formerly associate editor of *Smithsonian* magazine.

CLARENCE NERO is an MFA candidate at Louisiana State University. His first novel, *Cheekie: A Child Out of the Desire* was selected as "One of the Best First Novels of 1998," by *Library Journal*. He was a guest speaker at Maya Angelou's Life Writing Conference at Howard University, and his poetry has been published in the National Library of Poetry anthology, *Through the Hourglass*.

Bibliography

Als, Hilton. "Songbird: Maya Angelou Takes Another Look at Herself," *New Yorker*, 78:22 (2002 August 5), 72–76.

Arensberg, Liliane K. "Death as Metaphor of Self in *I Know Why the Caged Bird Sings*," *CLA Journal*, 20:2 (December 1976): 273–291.

Babb, Valerie. "Maya Angelou," *Langston Hughes Review*, 19 (Spring 2005): 1–81.

Benson, Carol. "Out of the Cage and Still Singing," *Writer's Digest* (January 1975): 18–20.

Bertolino, James. "Maya Angelou Is Three Writers: *I Know Why the Caged Bird Sings*," *Censored Books: Critical Viewpoints*. Ed. Nicholas J. Karolides, Lee Burress, and John M. Kean. Metuchen, NJ: The Scarecrow Press, 1993. pp. 299–305.

Bloom, Lynn Z. "Maya Angelou," *Dictionary of Literary Biography*, 38. Detroit: Gale, 1985. pp. 3–12.

Butterfield, Stephen. *Black Autobiography in America*. Amherst: University of Massachusetts Press, 1974.

Chrisman, Robert. "*The Black Scholar* Interviews Maya Angelou," *Black Scholar* (January–February 1977): 44–52.

Cole-Leonard, Natasha. "Maya Angelou's *Hallelujah! The Welcome Table, A Lifetime of Memories with Recipes* as Evocative Text, or, 'Ain't' Jemima's Recipes," *Langston Hughes Review*, 19 (Spring 2005): 66–69.

Cordell, Shirley J. "The Black Woman: A Focus on 'Strength of Character' in *I Know Why the Caged Bird Sings*," *Virginia English Bulletin*, 36:2 (Winter 1986): 36–39.

Demetrakopoulos, Stephanie A. "The Metaphysics of Matrilinearism in Women's Autobiography: Studies of Mead's *Blackberry Winter*, Hellman's *Pentimento*, Angelou's *I Know Why the Caged Bird Sings*, and Kingston's *The Woman Warrior*," in *Women's Autobiography: Essays in Criticism*. Ed. Estelle Jelinek. Bloomington: Indiana University Press, 1980. pp. 180–205.

Elliott, Jeffrey M., ed. *Conversations with Maya Angelou*. Jackson: University Press of Mississippi, 1989.

Estes-Hicks, Onita. "The Way We Were: Precious Memories of the Black Segregated South," *African American Review*, 27:1 (Spring 1993): 9–18.

Foster, Frances. "Parents and Children in Autobiography by Southern Afro-American Writers," *Home Ground: Southern Autobiography*. Columbia: University of Missouri Press, 1992. pp. 98–109.

Froula, Christine. "The Daughter's Seduction: Sexual Violence and Literary History," *Signs*, 11:4 (Summer 1986): 621–644.

Fulghum, Robert. "Home Truths and Homilies," *Washington Post Book World* (September 19, 1993): 4.

Gabbin, Joanne V. "Maya Angelou: The People's Poet Laureate: An Introduction," *Langston Hughes Review*, 19 (Spring 2005): 3–7.

Georgoudaki, Ekaterini, *Race, Gender, and Class Perspectives in the Works of Maya Angelou, Gwendolyn Brooks, Rita Dove, Nikki Giovanni, and Audre Lorde*. Thessaloniki: Aristotle University of Thessaloniki, 1991.

Gilbert, Susan. "Maya Angelou's *I Know Why the Caged Bird Sings:* Paths to Escape," *Mount Olive Review*, 1:1 (Spring 1987): 39–50.

Goodman, G., Jr. "Maya Angelou's Lonely Black Chick Outlook," *New York Times* (March 24, 1972): 28.

Gottlieb, Annie. "Growing Up and the Serious Business of Survival," *New York Times Book Review* (June 16, 1974): 16, 20.

Gruesser, John C. "Afro-American Travel Literature and Africanist Discourse," *Black American Literature Forum*, 24:1 (Spring 1990): 5–20.

Hord, Fred Lee. "Someplace to Be a Black Girl," *Reconstructing Memory: Black Literary Criticism*. Chicago: Third World Press, 1991. pp. 75–85.

Inge, Tonette Bond, ed. *Southern Women Writers: The New Generation*. Tuscaloosa: University of Alabama Press, 1990.

Kelly, Ernece B. Review of *I Know Why the Caged Bird Sings*, *Harvard Educational Review*, 40:4 (November 1970): 681–682.

Kent, George E. "Maya Angelou's *I Know Why the Caged Bird Sings* and Black Autobiographical Tradition," *Kansas Quarterly*, 7 (1975): 75–78. Reprinted in *African American Autobiography: A Collection of Critical Essays*. Ed. William L. Andrews. Englewood Cliffs, NJ: Prentice-Hall, 1993. pp. 162–170.

Kinnamon, Keneth. "Call and Response: Intertextuality in Two Autobiographical Works by Richard Wright and Maya Angelou," *Studies in Black American*

Literature, Vol. II: Belief vs. Theory in Black American Literary Criticism. Ed. Joe Weixlmann and Chester J. Fontenot. Greenwood, FL: Penkevill Publishing Co., 1986. pp. 121–134.

MacKethan, Lucinda H. "Mother Wit: Humor in Afro-American Women's Autobiography," *Studies in American Humor,* 4:1–2 (Spring 1985): 51–61.

Maierhofer, Roberta. "'Hold! Stop! Don't Pity Me': Age, Gender, and Ethnicity in American Studies," *Arbeiten aus Anglistik und Amerikanistik,* 25:1 (2000): 107–118.

Manora, Yolanda M. "'What You Looking at Me For? I Didn't Come to Stay': Displacement, Disruption, and Black Female Subjectivity in Maya Angelou's *I Know Why the Caged Bird Sings,*" *Women's Studies: An Interdisciplinary Journal,* 34:5 (2005 July–August): 359–375.

McMurry, Myra K. "Role-Playing as Art in Maya Angelou's *Caged Bird,*" *South Atlantic Bulletin,* 41:2 (May 1976): 106–111.

McPherson, Dolly. "Defining the Self through Place and Culture: Maya Angelou's *I Know Why the Caged Bird Sings,*" *MAWA Review,* 5:1 (June 1990): 12–14.

———. *Order Out of Chaos: The Autobiographical Works of Maya Angelou.* New York: Peter Lang, 1990.

Megna-Wallace, Joanne. "Simone de Beauvoir and Maya Angelou: Birds of a Feather," *Simone de Beauvoir Studies,* 6 (1986): 49–55.

Moore, Opal. "Learning to Live: When the Caged Bird Breaks From the Cage," *Censored Books: Critical Viewpoints.* Ed. Nicholas J. Karolides, Lee Burress, and John M. Kean. Metuchen, NJ: The Scarecrow Press, 1993. pp. 306–316.

Nero, Clarence. "A Discursive Trifecta: Community, Education, and Language in *I Know Why the Caged Bird Sings,*" *Langston Hughes Review,* 19 (Spring 2005): 61–65.

Phillips, Frank Lamont. Review of *Gather Together in My Name, Black World,* 24:9 (July 1975): 52, 61.

Premo, Cassie. "When the Difference Becomes Too Great: Images of the Self and Survival in a Postmodern World," *Genre,* 16 (1995): 183–191.

Redmond, Eugene B. "Boldness of Language and Breadth: An Interview with Maya Angelou," *Black American Literature Forum,* 22:2 (Summer 1988): 156–157.

Sample, Maxine. "Gender, Identity, and the Liminal Self: The Emerging Woman in Buchi Emecheta's *The Bride Price* and Maya Angelou's *I Know Why the Caged Bird Sings,*" in *North-South Linkages and Connections in Continental and Diaspora African Literatures,* edited by Edris Makward, Mark Lilleleht, and Ahmed Saber. Trenton, New Jersey: Africa World, 2005: pp. 213–225.

Saunders, James Robert. "Breaking Out of the Cage: The Autobiographical Writings of Maya Angelou," *Hollins Critic,* 28:4 (October 1991): 1–11.

Schramm, Katharina. "Imagined Pasts—Present Confrontations: Literary and Ethnographic Explorations into Explorations into Pan-African Identity

Politics," in *Africa, Europe, and (Post)Colonialism: Racism, Migration and Disapora in African Literatures,* edited by Susan Arndt and Marek Spitczok von Brisinski. Bayreuth, Germany: Bayreuth University, 2006: pp. 243–256.

Tate, Claudia, ed. *Black Women Writers at Work.* New York: Continuum, 1983. pp. 1–11.

Tawake, Sandra Kiser. "Multi-Ethnic Literature in the Classroom: Whose Standards?" *World Englishes: Journal of English as an International and Intranational Language,* 10:3 (Winter 1991): 335–340.

Tinnie, Wallis. "Maya Angelou," in *The History of Southern Women's Literature,* edited by Carolyn Perry, Mary Louise Weaks, and Doris Betts. Baton Rouge: Louisiana State University Press, 2002: pp. 517–524.

Vermillion, Mary. "Reembodying the Self: Representations of Rape in *Incidents in the Life of a Slave Girl* and *I Know Why the Caged Bird Sings,*" *Biography,* 15:3 (Summer 1992): 243–260.

Wall, Cheryl. "Maya Angelou," *Women Writers' Talking.* Ed. Janet Todd. New York: Holmes & Meier, 1983: pp. 59–67.

Weller, Sheila. "Work in Progress/Maya Angelou," *Intellectual Digest* (June 1973).

Acknowledgments

Lucinda H. MacKethan. "Mother Wit: Humor in Afro-American Women's Autobiography," *Studies in American Humor*, Volume 4, Numbers 1–2 (Spring–Summer 1985): pp. 51–61. Copyright © 1985 Lucinda H. MacKethan. Reprinted by permission of the author.

Shirley J. (S. J.) Cordell-Robinson. "The Black Woman: A Focus on 'Strength of Character' in *I Know Why the Caged Bird Sings*," *Virginia English Bulletin*, Volume 36, Number 2 (Winter 1986): pp. 36–39. Copyright © 1986 Shirley J. (S. J.) Cordell. Reprinted by permission of the author.

Carol E. Neubauer. "An Interview with Maya Angelou," *The Massachusetts Review*, Volume 28 (Summer 1987): pp. 286–292. Copyright © 1987 The Massachusetts Review. Reprinted by permission of the publisher.

Joanne Megna-Wallace. "Simode de Beauvoir and Maya Angelou: Birds of a Feather," *Simone de Beauvoir Studies*, Volume 6 (1989): pp. 49–55. Copyright © 1989 Simone de Beauvior Society. Reprinted by permission of the publisher.

Elizabeth Fox-Genovese. "Myth and History: Discourse of Origins in Zora Neale Hurston and Maya Angelou," *Black American Literature Forum*, Volume 24, Number 2 (Summer 1990): pp. 221–235. Copyright © 1990 Estate of Elizabeth Fox-Genovese. Reprinted by permission of the estate.

Bonnie Braendlin. "A (Sub)version of the American Dream in Maya Angelou's *I Know Why the Caged Bird Sings*," *Middle Atlantic Writers' association (MAWA) Review*, Volume 6, Number 1 (June 1991): pp. 4–6. Copyright © 1991 Bonnie Braendlin. Reprinted by permission of the author.

Ian Marshall. "Why the Caged Bird Laughs: Humor in Maya Angelou's *I Know Why the Caged Bird Sings*," *Middle Atlantic Writers' Association (MAWA) Review*, Volume 6, Number 1 (June 1991): pp. 7–10. Copyright © 1991 Ian Marshall. Reprinted by permission of the author.

Marcia Ann Gillespie. "Maya Angelou: Lessons in Living," *Essence*, Volume 23, Number 8 (December 1992): 48–52. Copyright © 1992 Marcia Ann Gillespie. Reprinted by permission of the author.

Onita Estes-Hicks. "The Way We Were: Precious Memories of the Black Segregated South," *African American Review*, Volume 27, Number 1 (Spring 1993): pp. 9–18. Copyright © 1993 Onita Estes-Hicks. Reprinted by permission of the author.

Cassie Premo-Steele. "When the Difference Becomes Too Great: Images of the Self and Survival in a Postmodern World," *Genre*, Volume 16 (1995): pp. 183–191. Copyright © 1995 Cassie Premo-Steele. Reprinted by permission of the author.

Dana Chamblee-Carpenter. "Searching for a Self in Maya Angelou's *I Know Why the Caged Bird Sings*," *Publications of the Mississippi Philological Association* (1996): pp. 6–12. Copyright © 1996 Dana Chamblee-Carpenter. Reprinted by permission of the author.

Siphokazi Koyana and Rosemary Gray. "Growing Up with Maya Angelou and Sindiwe Magona: A Comparison," *English in Africa*, Volume 29, Number 1 (May 2002): pp. 85–98. Copyright © 2002 Siphokazi Koyana and Rosemary Gray. Reprinted by permission of Rosemary Gray.

Lucinda Moore. "A Conversation with Maya Angelou at 75," *Smithsonian*, Volume 34, Number 1 (April 2003): p. 96. Copyright © 2003 Smithsonian Institution. Reprinted by permission of the publisher.

Clarence Nero. "A Discursive Trifecta: Community, Education, and Language in *I Know Why the Caged Bird Sings*," *The Langston Hughes Review*, Volume 19 (Spring 2005): pp. 61–65. Copyright © 2005 Langston Hughes Review. Reprinted by permission of the publisher.

Index